JUST
Thinking

C.J. DAKOTA

Studio Griffin
A Publishing Company
www.studiogriffin.net

For information, contact:
Studio Griffin
A Publishing Company
studiogriffin@outlook.com
www.studiogriffin.net

Cover Design by Ruth E. Griffin
Cover image generated by AI/Adobe

Permission statements for the use of various Bible translations listed in Appendix.

First Edition

ISBN-13: 978-1-954818-52-1

Library of Congress Control Number: 2024923778

1 2 3 4 5 6 7 8 9 10

This book is dedicated to my family
who encouraged and believed in me

Contents

Introduction

This book, **'Just Thinking,'** is a collection of a few meaningful subjects I have pondered over the years. It is not a single thought, and there was no planned continuity between the selected topics, all topics stand alone. I believe these thoughts are profound conclusions based on the truth revealed by the Word of God, the Bible. The conclusions laid out here have greatly influenced my life, and I believe these truths will have an equivalent impact on yours, if fully realized.

With sound logic and reasoning, we can derive from the scriptures indirect truths that go beyond the surface-level reading of the Word. Additionally, information is also revealed by the empowering Holy Spirit when we make it a practice to spend time meditating on the Word.

> *Keep this Book of the Law always on your lips; meditate on it day and night, so that you may be careful to do everything written in it. Then you will be prosperous and successful. Have I not commanded you? Be strong and courageous. Do not be afraid; do not be discouraged, for the Lord your God will be with you wherever you go. **Joshua 1:8-9 (NIV)***

There are single statements within the Word that are profound, invoking new perspectives, revelations, and concepts. If we yield to their implications, they are life-altering. I pray that this book reveals new truths to you; not only that but sparks a fire in your heart that can only be quenched by a new revelation of the importance of meditating on the Word. Learn to treasure each statement in the Word no matter how brief it is. A statement's importance isn't proportional to its length. No, a single word can be life-altering.

In addition, we have severely underestimated the need for knowing and understanding the schemes of Satan, for he is a master at deceiving. He is the source of evil in this world. This evil progresses throughout our society, through the hearts and wills of men with little resistance due to his uncanny ability to deceive. Therefore, we must give the proper weight to it and apply significant effort to combat it. The church as a whole has failed to do this, and the consequence of that failure is apparent. In Genesis, Satan deceived Eve with a simple distortion of the truth, now he deceives the world with his wiles.

> *Finally, my brethren, be strong in the Lord, and in the power of his might. Put on the whole armour of God, that ye may be able to stand against the **wiles** of the devil.*
> ***Ephesians 6:10-11 (KJV)***

The Great Commissioning Is The Mandatory Call for All

Most of us rise in the morning pushing forward as we walk into our lives. We have convinced ourselves that our lives have meaning for we are producing worldly things that bring pleasure, joy, improvement, or extend life. However, when we view this moment in time against eternity, our perspective drastically changes—an epiphany. Surely, what is an improved or extended life if it ends up in hell? What is joy or pleasure if it is temporary and eternal pain is in the forecast? There must be a recognition of one's current predicament and that of others in the light of eternity. With that epiphany fully grasped, how can we say we love others then passively observe them march toward hell and do nothing to warn them? Are we liars?

If we position anything in advance of God's commanded quest to spread the gospel, then the love of God hasn't penetrated our hearts. This is the implicit truth whether we confront it or not. The truth can't be veiled or diluted; we can only embrace it . The truth doesn't cease to exist, for it is immutable. The truth will set you free if you yield to it; if you ignore it, it will crush you.

The great commission is laid out in **Matthew 28:16-20.**
Verse 20 is clearly stated as a commandment.

> *Then the eleven disciples went to Galilee, to the mountain
> where Jesus had told them to go. When they saw him, they
> worshiped him; but some doubted. Then Jesus came to
> them and said, "All authority in heaven and on earth has
> been given to me. Therefore go and make disciples of all
> nations, baptizing them in the name of the Father and of
> the Son and the Holy Spirit,* **and teaching them to
> obey everything I have commanded you. And
> surely, I am with you always, to the very end of
> the age."** *(MSG)*

The commission does not require ministry credentials, only
obedience. Revelation 12:11 speaks of the power of our
testimony, when we are witnessing, our testimony is a very
effective tool.

I was once witnessing to a drug user who had been trying
diligently for years to overcome the habit. He said to me with
much anguish, "You do not understand my condition and I
don't want to hear anything you have to say."

Later, after I got over the initial shock, his perspective was
more than understandable. This is where a former drug user's
testimony would have been effective. The battles that we have
overcome with the help of the Holy Spirit can be used by the
spirit to help others. This is our testimony, and it is a very
powerful tool. Our life experiences with the Holy Spirit help us
to overcome the evils of this world. No drug user can deny the
power of the Holy Spirit to overcome drug addiction when
speaking to one who has done just that, one who empathizes
and fully understands.

*And we know that **all things work together for good** to those who love God, to those who are called according to His purpose. **Romans 8:28 (NKJV)***

As we put the Great Commission in the forefront of our spirit walk utilizing our testimony, we will be met with resistance and sometimes even a sense of satisfaction. With this satisfaction, we may feel a need to take a break. Please keep the break to a minimum. Experience has taught me there is no such thing as a pause in our ministry, we must always keep moving forward. So, the Great Commission is a lifelong never-ending pursuit. When we are active, we are producing fruit, but when we are static, we are more likely to stumble or move backward. When King David stopped going to war with his army, he committed adultery with Uriah's wife, Bathsheba (2 Samuel 11). When we are at war, we prepare. When we are not active, we relax; and what we fail to remember is we are always at war, for our enemy never sleeps.

One Must Carefully Choose Who One Emulates

Christ is the one we should seek to emulate, there is not better model. But, for some in their earnest pursuit to spread the gospel, they will seek to emulate another, searching for one with a large church. But they forget that Jesus may have been in the crowd, but he was not a fraction of it—he ministered to it.

In our society, it is believed that the larger the count within the church building, the greater the ministry. With that criterion, Jesus' ministry appears to be a little anemic. Some people will never enter a church building, especially now with the current level of hypocrisy. Jesus went directly to the people and their needs. This is the model he set for us: to lead, by example; on-the-job training. The church body isn't confined within the walls of a building—no, it is society itself.

The one you should seek to emulate will be a loner with a few close acquaintances, scorned, eccentric, laughed at, hated, unworldly but committed, peaceful, determined, faithful, and fruitful. His light will be exceedingly bright, but most will not see it due to Satan's deceptions. It appears to be an enormous blunder, an ark resting on dry land. Why? Because most are unaware that the rain is coming. As the last trumpet sounds, the door to the ark is shut and only those who can hear, hear it. The flood was the same event for the believer as well as the non-believer—for one it is a life-ending catastrophe, and for the other, salvation. The trumpet is sounding now, but it is in the distance and traveling towards us, can you hear it?

Emulate the person who is building an ark by building alongside him. Those bent on salvation will be coming to him; two-by-two, the Great Commission will be his light. Those around him will be protected and calm, not full of strife. He will glorify the Holy One of Israel, and he will be an outsider, for he will not be in the world. His ways will seem foolish by worldly standards, unpopular and serene.

For the foolishness of God is wiser than man's wisdom, and the weakness of God is stronger than man's strength. Brothers, think of what you were when you were called. Not many of you were wise by human standards; not many were influential; not many were of noble birth. 1 Corinthians 1:25 (NIV)

The Love Of This World Is A Thief, For It Steals So Much From Us

*"Do not lay up for yourselves treasures on earth, where moth and rust destroy and where thieves break in and steal, but lay up for yourselves treasures in heaven, where neither moth nor rust destroys and where thieves do not break in and steal. For where your treasure is, there your heart will be also." **Matthew 6:19-20 (NKJV)***

Some will work sacrificially seeking only to hear the Father say, "Well done, my good and faithful servant," When these words are spoken, all their worldly sacrifices attract the Father's attention. Then the Father bestows on them incomprehensible treasures, all in the context of eternity.

Alternatively, some give their lives to God but lack love and consequently produce little to no fruit, focusing entirely on the demands of this brief worldly existence for they love the world and the pleasures it brings. They may enter heaven but when the time comes for rewards to be presented, they receive silence from the Almighty, and then their costly worldly ambitions explode into a deafening sound for all to hear. This scenario is explicitly outlined in the Parable of the Sower **(Matthew 13:1-23).** Pay close attention to the group whose harvest is laced with thorns that choke out the good crop.

As youths, we are impatient and seek immediate gratification. Many times, this is at the expense of long-term success. For example, one may save money to buy a car. As soon as enough money is saved to purchase a low-end unreliable car, it is spent. Because the car is unreliable, the purchase only has a short life span. If patience is practiced, a more reliable and long-term car purchase can be obtained.

It is like this when we sacrifice worldly accomplishments for eternal treasures. God gave the standard that we should seek the maximum treasures.

> *Jesus answered him, "If you wish to be perfect [that is, have the spiritual maturity that accompanies godly character with no moral or ethical deficiencies], go and sell what you have and give [the money] to the poor, and you will have treasure in heaven; and come, follow Me [becoming My disciple, believing and trusting in Me and walking the same path of life that I walk]." **Matthew 19:21 (AMP)***

I don't know of anyone who has sacrificed that much outside of Jesus; I know I have not. However, that is our standard. Couple Matthew 19:21 with Mark 12:42,43 (KJV):

> *For whosoever shall **give** you a **cup of water** to drink in **my name**, because ye belong to Christ, verily I say unto you, he shall not lose his reward.*

You see, the simplest effort is rewarded but we sacrifice it all in the pursuit of worldly gratification. When I review my life in this light, it is hard not to cry uncontrollably.

Which is more valuable, a career as a lawyer with a seven-figure salary that evolves into a congressional seat; or an overseas missionary position that started at sixteen years of age, never ended until death, and lived in absolute Godly obedience? The career produces worldly authority, a lavish lifestyle, travel, multiple homes, many cars, and wide worldly recognition, only to burn up in the fire on the day of judgment, while the latter produces so much eternal treasure that no one can conceive it.

As Christians, many of us will spend our lives seeking after the former; we buy lottery tickets wishing for and even praying for it. The funny thing is the latter is achievable by all, it just requires a will.

> *"Again, the kingdom of heaven is like a merchant looking for fine pearls. When he found one of great value, he went away and sold everything he had and bought it.* **Matthew 13:45-46 (NIV)**

Some may think the preceding verses imply that earthly gifts are given when you find the Kingdom of Heaven—how short sighted. No, heavenly gifts are given, eternal gifts. It is called the Kingdom of Heaven, not the Kingdom of Earth.

The Deceptions Of Satan

The devil has a multitude of deceptive schemes. He is brilliant, and his knowledge far exceeds ours. He is our adversary, and we are no match for him. Let that sink in for a second.

Fortunately, Jesus has supplied us with his Word to use as an anchor for the truth. He also gives us wisdom and the Holy Spirit to guide us. With that combination, we can stand against the devil's schemes.

However, so many of us rely on our own understanding and reasoning. When we do, we become ripe victims of the devil's schemes. We all have fallen into his deceptions; the question is to what degree.

As new believers, we believe that Satan's deceptions are easily detectable, and obvious and impact a few. The more we grow in Christ though, the more we realize that Satan's deceptions are too numerous to count and far-reaching; countries, governments, churches, social groups, people groups, etc., are all victims of them. None escapes their grasp. Believers who believe they have succumbed only to a few deceptions or have a firm mastery over Satan's deceptions are the most deceived of all. For the wise knows he has been deceived by much and is in a constant state to find other deceptions he is currently unaware of.

As a result of succumbing to a multitude of deceptions, many followers of Christ interpret the scriptures incorrectly and consequently walk paths contrary to the will of God. This is because they do not approach God's Word objectively; they adhere to logical fallacies, faulty perceptions, unrealized biases, worldly traditions, unhealthy preconceptions, etc. All of which can be easily remedied with a little bout of listening. Unfortunately, arrogance fits into this equation as well.

Occasionally in our lives, we experience a life-changing event. The event doesn't have to be traumatic but just painful enough to etch it into your long-term memory. One such event occurred while I was in high school taking an advanced math course. I was very good with mathematics; some would call me a curve buster. I realized once I got a little older why this particular teacher gave us work beyond what was expected for the course. He was seeking to get the most out of us, setting no boundaries. I greatly appreciate his efforts now, but not so much then. As most teachers do now, they teach within the boundaries set by the school and not pushing the students beyond their limits. If you don't push them past their limits, how do you know where the limits are?

Back in the classroom, it was common for us to have exams where a curve was invoked for the average score, which was less than impressive. In one such case, he gave us two exams at once. After a couple of days, the exams were graded, and the results were in. Before he distributed the exams, unfortunately, he announced that there would be no curve adjustments because he had 'A+' scores on both exams. The average exam score was in the sixties. However, I received a 100 and a 105.

There was a bonus question on the second exam worth 10 points meaning that I had missed a problem worth less than the bonus. I reviewed my results and was convinced that the problem that my teacher marked incorrectly was an error on his part. I arrogantly walked up to his desk and challenged him. I was wrong and was humiliated in front of the class.

I learned that day and I learned it well: even if you are good at something and convinced you are right, you can still be wrong. Also, arrogance will always make you look foolish in any setting, and the greater the assertion of your arrogance, the greater your foolishness will be exposed. Being exceptionally skilled doesn't make you wise, it just makes it easier for you to be arrogant. Being convinced that you are right just means you are more likely not to listen.

A wise person would have asked the teacher to explain the problem they missed. If we could only entertain the idea that we possibly could be wrong, we could learn to be right. If we could set aside our pride, God can correct us. To not yield to deception, we must be willing to embrace a strike against our pride. This is the same pride that looks for immediate gratification by seeking approval from the world. Remember, we forfeit God's approval when we seek the world's approval.

> *"Be careful not to practice your righteousness in front of others to be seen by them. If you do, you will have no reward from your Father in heaven. "So when you give to the needy, do not announce it with trumpets, as the hypocrites do in the synagogues and on the streets, to be honored by others. Truly I tell you, they have received their reward in full. But when you give to the needy, do not let your left hand know what your right hand is doing, so that your giving may be in secret. Then your Father, who sees what is done in secret, will reward you.* **Matthew 6:1-5 (NIV)**

There are processes where God humbles us. These lessons learned make us slow to speak and quick to listen. One means by which God does this is by revealing deceptions that we have fallen prey to. Quick listening is a behavior that one learns when knowing they aren't immune to being deceived.

For those who haven't learned this lesson, they give their opinions without the slightest reservation or hesitation, and they give their opinion frequently with bold confidence. As the scriptures state,

> *A fool does not delight in understanding, only in airing his opinion. Proverbs 18:2 (BSB)*

An opportunity to learn presents itself when we listen attentively and allow the other person to fully present their point. If we attempt to formulate a rebuttal while their point is being presented, we diminish the possibility of learning. Listening isn't as simple as it appears at first thought—it requires discipline. A person who listens well also learns well. Poor listeners live in their own derived worldview, which he/she believes is flawless, and are sure of their conclusions. A poor listener lives in a sea of deceptions. Why can I say that? If a person is aware of the magnitude of deceptions and knows how vulnerable people are to these deceptions, one would be quick to listen. No one walks through a minefield hastily relying on his own ability to discern potential danger, especially if others have traveled through the minefield already. No, he listens attentively.

Most believe we are living close to the coming of the end of the age. Jesus' disciples asked him when the end of the age would come, and **Matthew 24:4** captures his response.

> *And as he sat upon the mount of Olives, the disciples came unto him privately, saying, Tell us, when shall*

these things be? and what shall be the sign of thy coming,
and of the end of the world?
And Jesus answered and said unto them, Take heed that
no man deceive you.(KJV)

Jesus's first mentioned in his characterization of the end of the age was to warn men not to be deceived. It is prudent we heed this warning.

Prophecy, Parables, And The Mysteries Of God

Prophecy

There is a special blessing for understanding Revelation, the book of prophecy.

> *"'BLESSED is he who reads and those who hear the words of this prophecy, and keep those things which are written in it; for the time is near."* ***(Revelation 1:3)***

As you can see, this verse was included at the very beginning of the book of Revelation. I believe the Holy Spirit put it in that location for us to realize the importance of the prophecies that are to follow and for us to give it its appropriate attention. One-third of the Bible is prophetic, yet many will discard prophecy for failure to understand its value. God establishes prophetic patterns that repeat themselves in future events. This allows us to know what to expect in particular situations and to anticipate and prepare for known outcomes. The book of Revelations is an aggregation of prophecies presented throughout the Bible; this is another reason why the entire Bible needs to be consumed. To fully understand the book of Revelation, one needs to understand all the subcomponents found throughout the Bible. Although it was written by forty different authors, it is one cohesive book, arranged by the Holy Spirit.

Parables

Why did Jesus speak in parables?

> *Jesus replied, "Because they haven't received the **secrets** of the kingdom of heaven, but you have." "For those who have will receive more and they will have more than enough." "But as for those who don't have, even the little they have will be taken away from them." "This is why I speak to the crowds in parables: although they see, they don't really see; and although they hear, they don't really hear or understand." **Matthew 13:11-13 (CEB)***

The first sentence of the scriptures refers to the **secrets** of the kingdom, a necessary prerequisite. If you don't know what they are, this should be a very high priority for you to ascertain them.

Kingdom of Heaven

Jesus spoke about the Kingdom of Heaven more than any other topic. Most people would immediately say He spoke more about the cross, but the good news of the cross was not preached until after the resurrection. Jesus always cloaked the kingdom in parables. What is the kingdom and why did he cloak it? Most Christians think salvation and the Kingdom of Heaven are synonymous, but are they? Salvation is not hidden, and it is simple and easy to understand. Remember, Jesus said, a person will sell everything he has to obtain the Kingdom. (Matthew 13:44).

Mystery

Read the third chapter of Ecclesiastes and you will agree that God has put into each of our hearts a desire to seek beyond ourselves for a deeper meaning of life. We all know intuitively that there is more than just this world; also, afore knowledge that there is an eternity. It is this desire that drives us to seek out the mysteries of God.

> *"It is the glory of God to conceal a thing, but the honor of* **kings** *is to search out a matter."* **Proverbs 25:2 (AMP)**

I have come to learn that prophecy, parables, and God's mysteries all work together. They complement each other and all three are required for full Biblical understanding. Surface-level reading of the Word will not reveal the hidden treasures that these three provide. It takes study, meditation, and the Holy Spirit. You must read and understand the Bible in its entirety. Why do I say that? For the mysteries of God span throughout the Word; it relies on an understanding of concepts that grasp the big picture.

Let's tackle a short passage and amass what we can with a surface-level approach, then dive a little deeper into the passage and see what more we can glean from the text. This passage is a conversation between Jesus and the Pharisees and their attempt to trap Him into saying something that would be in opposition to Caesar's rule.

Then went the Pharisees and took counsel on how they might entangle him in his talk.

> *And they sent out unto him their disciples with the Herodians, saying, Master, we know that thou art true, and teachest the way of God in truth, neither carest thou for any man: for thou regardest not the person of men. Tell us, therefore, What thinkest thou? Is it lawful to give tribute unto Caesar, or not?*

But Jesus perceived their wickedness, and said, Why tempt ye me, ye hypocrites?
Shew me the tribute money. And they brought unto him a penny.
And he saith unto them, Whose is this image and superscription?
They say unto him, Caesar's. Then saith he unto them, Render therefore unto Caesar the things which are Caesar's; and unto God the things that are God's.
When they had heard these words, they marveled, and left him, and went their way. **Luke 20:16-22 (KJV)**

In verse 17, the Pharisees asked Jesus if it was lawful to give tribute to Caesar expecting Jesus to state that you should honor the Father and not man.

Jesus's response was to give to Caesar what belonged to him and to give God what belonged to him. On the surface, there is no conflict here; one isn't placed above the other. However, the Pharisees knew it had greater meaning, and they knew why Jesus used an image to orchestrate his message. First, who is created in the image of God, man? So, Jesus was stating, give to God what belongs to God knowing that all belongs to God, even Caesar, and all that Caesar possesses belongs to God as well. Plus, per God's Word, we are not allowed to make graven images of anything from Heaven. Ceasar's image was on the coin, which is fine as long as Caesar isn't claimed to be a deity. The Pharisees claimed to be followers of God, therefore Caesar, whom they wanted to give tribute to, could not be a deity but a man. Otherwise, the people would have stoned the Pharisees if they had claimed Caesar was anything other than a man. To derive this deeper meaning, one needed to have been familiar with Genesis which revealed that man is made in God's image; plus, Deuteronomy, and the commandments that address the restriction of making images of heavenly beings.

The lack of knowledge of the entire Bible is one of the reasons why I believe so many have struggled over the book of Revelation, myself included. The symbolisms and patterns revealed in the book of Revelation are disclosed in the prophetic text within the Old Testament, while the understanding of parables provides some of the structure needed and the mysteries fill in the gaps and provide illumination.

First, we need to know that rightfully understanding prophecy comes with a blessing. If God provides a blessing for completing a task, you can be assured the task is well worth the effort. Second, it is the honor of kings to search out a matter. Why is it the honor of **kings** and not just anyone? That is a mystery within itself. Third, the secrets of the Kingdom of Heaven must be received to fully understand parables.

The Cross

I don't believe we will fully comprehend what was accomplished on the Cross until we are in the presence of the Father. To better understand the Cross, we must be aware of our condition without it and then understand the opportunities that are presented to us because of it. The scriptures say, *"all have sinned and come short of the glory of God"* Romans 3:23. So, we will face judgment by an infinitely Holy and righteous God. What is the price we must pay? A righteous God cannot ignore sin, he must judge it, or he will cease to be righteous. Our judgment is infinite for we have sinned against an infinite God. Therefore, Hell is justified because of who God is. If you don't grasp that, then you do not fully comprehend the Holiness and righteousness of the God you serve.

Let me explain it this way, even sinful men dispense different punishments for crimes depending on who it was committed against. If one slaps a neighbor while the disorderly neighbor is drunk, then the police may ignore the crime and send both men home. However, if one slaps a policeman, he may have a brief stay in the city jail. If that same person slaps the President, he is likely to go to prison. Same crime, different judgments, all due to who the crime was perpetrated against. With that in mind, what is the price of a sin committed against God?

Some have rejected the notion that there is a Hell, but how can one reject Hell for its severity but accept Heaven? If you don't think mankind deserves Hell, you must reject Heaven as well, for we would not deserve it either.

Now mercy is not getting the punishment you deserve. So, the Cross provides infinite mercy. Grace, on the other hand, is getting something that you have not earned. Like Hell, Heaven is infinite. If the gift is infinite, then grace is infinite. Who received grace makes a difference as well. Giving grace to Mother Teresa is different than giving grace to Hitler. We are all multitudes eviler to God than Hitler was to us. Consider this, would you give paradise to Hitler if he repented?

> But because of his great love for us, God, who is rich in mercy, made us alive with Christ even when we were dead in transgressions—it is by grace you have been saved. And God raised us up with Christ and seated us with him in the heavenly realms in Christ Jesus, **Ephesians 2:5-7 (NIV)**

So, mercy removes the judgment of God from us, but it doesn't provide an infinite gift. The infinite gift comes from grace.

The cost requires a perfect sacrifice that endures undeserving punishment without mercy so we can have mercy. It required a perfect soul, unblemished by sin, willingly self-sacrificed, whose value is infinite so you can enjoy grace. He received no mercy, the completely innocent one. The one who needed no grace for he had it all and he laid it all down.

So, what is the Cross? The Cross is where infinite mercy meets infinite grace, motivated by agape love. In the light of eternity, it provides a path where the justified hell-bound sinner can repent and then go to the undeserved Heaven, all while satisfying the righteousness requirements of our Holy Father. That, my friend, is simply amazing.

The Trinity

Our God is three in one: the Father, Son, and the Holy Spirit. This concept is rejected by many, some have even altered the Bible to remove the concept. The word Trinity isn't in the Bible, but the concept of the Trinity is explicitly seen.

> *In the beginning was the Word, and the Word was with God, and the Word was God. He was with God in the beginning. Through him all things were made; without him, nothing was made that has been made. In him was life, and that life was the light of all mankind. The light shines in the darkness, and the darkness has not overcome it. The Word became flesh and made his dwelling among us. We have seen his glory, the glory of the one and only Son, who came from the Father, full of grace and truth.* **John 1:1-5 and 14 (NIV)**

These verses identify the Son and his relationship with the Father, so much so that Jehovah's Witnesses altered the wording to fit their beliefs.

The funny thing is, with a little thought and sound reasoning, the Trinity is self-evident. First, let's identify a few characteristics of God; he is loving, trustworthy, faithful, personable, and all-knowing. Let's address the all-knowing: if this is true, God can't learn, for there is nothing he doesn't know. If the Trinity is not true, then I ask, before man and the angels were created, who did God love, who was he faithful to, how was he trustworthy, how was he personable? If the Trinity is not true, then the Son and the Holy Spirit were created and then God started manifesting relational characteristics—God grew. And if he grew, then originally, he wasn't all 'n' all.

You see, within the Trinity, all that is bound to relationships is sprouted. Since God can't learn or grow, then the Trinity has always been. John 1:3 supports what I just said: all that was created was accomplished by the Word. This would be impossible if the Word was created, he could not create himself. If the Father created the Word, then verse 1:3 is not true. Also, John 1:1 states that the *"Word was with God, and the Word was God."*

The closest man comes to the concept of the Trinity is man's relationship between the mind, spirit, and body. If I were to remove my mind and place it in a computer, could it not be said, in the beginning, was the computer operating system, and the operating system was with me and the computer operating system was me, it was with me from the beginning? As long as the communication links between the body, mind, and spirit remain unbroken, I will continue being me. It is a crude analogy with many flaws, but it may help you better understand the Trinity.

We are finite mortal men trying to understand the Creator. I can't understand life for it is incomprehensible and if I wasn't alive, I wouldn't believe it. I know God created me, but who am I? I'm asking that question from both a metaphysical and a self-aware perspective. I am self-aware but how can that be? The answer to that has escaped me; nevertheless, I am here.

How is thought generated, and how does it move things? The brain sends an electrical pulse to the muscle and the muscle, in turn, moves. This is true; however, the thought comes first, and it manipulates the brain. No person fully understands this thought's data to the brain transfer, it is so beyond us that no one can even conceive a workable theory. But each of us is indeed living proof.

The Trinity is true, and we can't discard it because we don't fully understand it, no more than we can discard the thought. After all, we don't fully understand how thought works either. Like thought, we know it exists and I know the Trinity exists. It is the arrogance of man that denies it and to even go as far as to change the Word of God. What arrogance. You don't have to physically alter the written Word of God to change it, you can teach something other than what is written.

In short, a personable God who requires relationships must have always existed. Never has God been impersonal. Therefore, the Trinity has always existed.

Why Does God Not Fully Reveal Himself To Mankind?

If God fully revealed himself, he would eliminate our ability to choose him over sin. Consider this: God tears the fabric of the sky, emerges from the tear, proceeds to earth, and this is witnessed by all. His existence at that point would be absolute. All would follow him, not because they love God but because there would be no alternative. The third of the angels that shadowed Satan when he tumbled proves this, for they existed in a perfect sinless environment and were fully aware of God in all his glory. When some of the angels were presented with a choice to sin, they did so. Before the fall of Satan, all the angels abided in God and committed no sins, yet one-third did not love God, for none that loved God would willingly depart from him. These angels appeared to be perfect beings but only God knew truly what was in their hearts. Their lack of love would have never been exposed without the opportunity to choose sin.

Humanity, on the other hand, is born into sin and through the gift of salvation can go where angels tread. Those that love the Lord, choose him and repent. When we live in eternity with the Lord, the choice to sin will be removed. Our past will be erased from our minds and eternity will be devoid of sin. The choice to choose sin will be no longer required since we have already chosen God in our earthly lives. Now eternity will be filled with only lovers of God. God has skillfully used sin to reveal the hearts of angels and men.

In the millennia (Revelation 20:4, God will rule the world from Jerusalem. Mortal children will be born during this time and life spans will be greatly enhanced. Men will be given the same opportunity as the angels by being in an environment led by God, but they must be allowed to choose God as well. Otherwise, like the angels that followed Satan, those who lack love would not be exposed. Therefore, Satan is released at the end of the millennia to present sin to the children that were born during the millennia. They will also have the history of mankind to learn from.

One last thing to consider: there is a good reason we must observe the ugliness of this world and endure its pain and suffering. Exposure to the consequences of sin better prepares us to make the correct choice. This is the main reason why the church grows more during persecution than it does during prosperity. If we lived in a perfect sinless world, unaware of the consequences of sin, would we choose God or depart like a third of the angels? No one can truly answer that question. We all hope we will make the correct choice, but I'm not inclined to bet my eternal soul. From my perspective, this ugly world with all its death, pain, and suffering is a blessing, for it allows me to appreciate the product of sin.

We can also derive from this scenario that agape love is something we choose, and it is not forced on us. We are commanded to choose it; its source is God. Deny the source and there is only Hell. This is why fallen angels are pure evil, they lack agape love.

Sound Reasoning
And Logic

Our society has discontinued using sound reasoning and logic to guide us in our thinking. Logical fallacies go unrecognized in the public media along with their many incorrect conclusions. The study of logic and its fallacies needs to be a mandatory course for all students, and it needs to be taught as early in their school years as possible. This would strike a major blow to Satan and his many deceptions.

I have drawn this statement from a scientific book: "Thought is an illusion, the brain tricks one into believing he is thinking." If that isn't a self-defeating statement, I have never heard one. The only way one can come to a statement like that is when he believes that nothing exists outside of the physical. Why does the writer bother writing the statement? If thinking is an illusion, why attempt to appeal to a listener who can't think? Next, how could he come to any conclusions, by his own words, for his thinking is an illusion?

There is a multitude of statements throughout the scientific community just like this one, all riddled with logical fallacies. Here is one of my favorites: "There is no absolute truth, truth is relative." That very statement could not be true if all truth was relative.

Here is another, individuals writing thick books on the meaninglessness of life. Figure that one out.

I'm only bringing these often-unnoticed fallacies to the surface so we can observe how the crème of the scientific community concocts poor logical statements constantly, right in public view, never to be called out, but to be blindly followed by the masses. With this in mind, we need to be careful not to allow the arrogance of men with their illogical statements to guide us away from the truth.

I have listened to political debates during the election for public offices. Those who participate in the debate are highly informed, and well-educated. Nevertheless, logical fallacies are used, never to be called out by their opponent, the media, or the audience. Consequently, wrong conclusions are realized and supported by the people. When I present these fallacies to many, they are often rejected. Although they are clearly understood, sometimes intuitively, they are rejected because the consequences are undesirable.

I have been told a statement similar to this one many times: "I know what you are saying is right, I can't prove you are wrong, but I can't believe it."

So, sound logic and reasoning only work when one is willing to accept another view, otherwise, it falls on deaf ears.

> *For the time will come when people will not put up with sound doctrine. Instead, to suit their own desires, they will gather around them a great number of teachers to say what their itching ears want to hear. They will turn*

their ears away from the truth and turn aside to myths.
2 Timothy 3:3-4 (NIV)

That verse would be hard to accept if I hadn't witnessed it myself.

The Infinite Monkey Theorem

The Infinite Monkey Theorem is a proposition that an unlimited number of monkeys, given typewriters and sufficient time, will eventually produce a particular text, such as Hamlet or even the complete works of Shakespeare.

This theorem has been used for decades to support evolution; the vast majority of the population never challenged but accepted it even though it is hopelessly flawed. The proposition says that with enough time even the most complex can be randomly realized. For example, dinosaurs evolved into the birds that you see today. With this theorem, the scientist could take their magic wand and hover it over the dinosaurs to the birds' transition period and make the impossible possible.

Let's scrutinize the theorem and expose its obvious flaws. The first stage in evolution, represented by the monkeys, is trying to produce a complex design from randomness. This is represented by authoring a complex book. However, a book must have an alphabet and where does the alphabet come from? The alphabet on the typewriter keys must be created by a mind, designed. An "A" is an "A" because someone says when these marks are arranged to form an "A", it is a letter of the English alphabet; otherwise, it is just random marks with no value.

With evolution, matter exists, and the mind comes from matter. This is bogus but for the sake of this argument, let's say it is possible. So, the theorem must be adjusted by removing any mind-produced objects. So, there can be no alphabets on the typewriter keys. Second, for writings with no alphabet to have any value, there must be a predefined language. Again, this requires a mind to develop one. If the book is written in Spanish, Spanish must be developed. Therefore, language is not allowed for the same reason the alphabets are not—it requires a mind. Lastly, someone needs to read the book, which requires a mind. So, let's rewrite the theorem without the use of design—in other words, a mind.

The Infinite Monkey Theorem is a proposition that an unlimited number of monkeys, given typewriters with no alphabets on the keys but random markings and sufficient time, will eventually produce a particular text, such as Hamlet or even the complete works of Shakespeare. It will be written in a non-alphabet-based, unknowable language, and interpreted by a mindless being. And with that theorem, they can have all the time they need—let's make it a zillion centuries.

I know the evolutionist will attack my interpretation of the removal of design, but the analogy is correct. The evolutionist has a problem: matter can't produce a mind. If it is true, please give me one viable theory.

In a few movies like the "Terminator", computers become self-aware magically. That demonstrates that there isn't a viable theory, or the writers would have used it.

The theorem was to provide the evolutionist with the ability to create the complex from randomness. It was their way to invoke design under the guise of randomness and time. Design only comes from the mind. The greater the complexity, the more intelligence is required. Look at the complexity of the universe, from the mere components of an atom to the galaxy, and design is implicit. The big bang theory only addresses the components necessary to form the universe, it can't address the interactions between the components.

Take a man for an example: if it was possible for a man to evolve from a single organism, how could earth's ecosystem with all the other animals and plants evolve as well and then form a cohesive system? This doesn't even take into account the complexity of man's internal biome. Without God, the matter has to create the design that we see, and no magic wand can bridge that gap.

> *The heavens declare the glory of God;*
> *the skies proclaim the work of his hands.*
> *Day after day they pour forth speech;*
> *night after night they reveal knowledge.*
> *They have no speech, they use no words; no sound is*
> *heard from them.*
> *Yet their voice goes out into all the earth, their words to*
> *the ends of the world*
> **Psalms 19:1-6 (NIV)**

Psalms 19 addresses the macro world; men were not aware of the micro world at the time of psalms were written. The Holy Spirit chose not to address it. This is my version of the psalms addressing the micro world:

> *The microscopic declares the glory of God;*
> *the information they exhibit proclaims the works of his*
> *mind.*

*Microsecond after microsecond they pour forth data;
quantum particle after quantum particle reveals his
intelligence.*
*They have no speech; they use no words; no sound is
heard from them.*
*Yet their voice goes throughout the scientific
community, their words to the ends of our thoughts.*

Why Does Evidence Fail To Persuade Us?

What I have come to recognize is that we choose to believe what we covet. All the evidence in the world can't overpower that desire. If you wish to believe there is no God, you will search out all the evidence needed to support it. Even if the evidence is flawed, the mind can disregard what it doesn't desire. This is a failing of the flesh, so it requires much attention. I have never convinced an atheist to believe in God and I have tried numerous times. However, I have seen atheists sprint to God when they choose to seek him. All the insurmountable proof that supported their atheism was promptly ignored. This is beautiful,; no obstruction can prevent one from reaching God if he sincerely seeks him. When speaking to an atheist or anyone with their particular beliefs, the answer we should be seeking is why they desire to believe.

Oprah once said that she could not believe in a God that was jealous. She also said, "There are many ways to God, there just can't be one way." What Oprah is articulating is the God she seeks to serve is one that she designs, one that has the characteristics and behaviors she so desires. We have to look past the assertion that is offered to us and ask why it was adamantly asserted. Why is jealousy unacceptable? Why must there be multiple ways? Isn't one way enough?

You can witness these types of biases during a football game. For instance, there can be a close referee-controlled call on the field and both sides of the team's fans witness it. The fans of one team will see it in their favor and the other team's fans will see it in their favor. Even if the play can be seen on the big screen, it will mostly fail to overcome the fans' bias.

As a society, we have come to accept that man is not capable of overpowering one's internal biases. Therefore, juries are selected, and judges are recused, for the average person bows to it.

At times, I have failed to adhere to that knowledge and waste significant time trying to convince a biased person to see past their biases. It can be difficult knowledge to yield to, but it is one, for the sake of time, we need to yield to it.

What I have learned is that we must address our own biases. We can't ignore them, or we become victims of the devil's schemes. For if one can't view evidence unbiasedly, he can't view the truth.

First, we need to be aware of our biases. Let us say we have a political party we support. We will tend to agree with its leadership. Remember, if our biases go unchecked, evidence will have little effect on us. When evidence is presented that supports our party, we will quickly accept it; when it opposes it, we will discard it. We desire to fit into the box that the party has created for us; we will feel comfortable there, and it is where we belong.

To incapacitate this bias, we must be objective when viewing the evidence. Use the Word of God as an anchor. Does it agree with God's Word, if it doesn't it is wrong. Our failing nature will want to justify the wrong by finding a greater wrong, especially if it is the adversary. It can be easy to accept the wrong if it's surrounded by things we desire. This is one of the devil's tactics, he gives us what we desire and then adds a small poison to the mix. The poison is usually a direct attack against God, an attack against a foundational truth that will cause severe damage. The damage is usually progressive like leaven in flour—with time the whole loaf is destroyed. We shouldn't trade benefits and desires that suit us and give the devil a strike at a foundational truth. That trade isn't in our best interest, it is shortsighted and selfish.

Know your personal biases, compensate for them, learn to be objective when viewing the evidence, and be aware of the devil's schemes. Let us not lie to ourselves and say we do not have biases or believe we have them in check. It takes continuous and considerable effort to compensate for our biases.

Dreams

I have dreams that are filled with symbolism, and the messages received from these dreams have changed the paths I was traveling on many occasions. I expected I avoided many pitfalls due to obedience.

I remember one experience vividly. A partner in the ministry had the vision to go to an adjacent city to start a tent revival. We discussed it in detail and were in the process of formulating the plans. I was excited and looking forward to God moving in a mighty way. The partner was going to be the primary leader; I was to follow his lead. I agreed and was ready to set sail. Shortly after we got to this stage of the effort, I had a dream. The dream told me to abandon the ministry. "It is not as it appears. You are latching on to an individual who is deceitful and not what he appears to be on the surface." This was completely uninspected, but I did pray for guidance and direction, and I received it. I accepted and adhered to God's will for He knows best.

My friend replaced me with another and continued his tent/sidewalk ministry. A few years later, his hidden personality traits surfaced, and the ministry eventually collapsed but not until the damage was done. His motivation was not in alignment with God's. The description I received from the dream couldn't have been better. A catastrophe was avoided.

Although these dreams are few and far between, my dreams are always packed with vital information that requires days to unravel. The key here is the dreams are packed with Biblical symbolism. I believe God uses symbolism because a large amount of data can be transferred quickly, and we are better inclined to remember images. Our minds are constantly busy, even when we are meditating on the Word. Rarely are our minds idle. With that thought, in a dream state, God has our full attention. This is called REM sleep. There are a few things we must master for dreams to be effective. We need to be aware of when God is speaking to us. For me, I just know. Have you ever felt when there is someone in your dream and you know who they are, but you can't see their face; that knowledge is just downloaded to you? Well, it is like that with me, I know because he tells me. I dream mostly in black and white, but dreams from God are always in color. Once the dream is over, I immediately wake up and write down what I saw and heard, leaving nothing out. You must record the dream immediately, do not wait until morning or you may forget key elements. If there are Biblical symbols, describe them and keep the sequential order of the dream. I say this because there will be additional revelations based on sequential order and the details of the symbols. With that information, the Bible, and much prayer, you can interpret the dream.

I hear people say that God never talks to them in dreams, but I believe he does, and they are not aware he is speaking. They believe it is another ordinary meaningless dream. They haven't learned to hear His voice. They know very little of the Word when reading the Bible, they give little attention to prophecy and symbolism and the patterns God has established. Everything in the Bible is there for a reason, I mean everything; nothing is by chance.

This is how I became aware that God was speaking to me via dreams. I had a few dreams, but I didn't think much of them. I discarded them but the dreams seemed to linger in my mind for days. Plus, when the dreams were happening, the environment was intense and unique, and I knew they were special. Still, it didn't set off any bells. When I was later studying the Word, I came across a few symbols, and they were described in the Word. These symbols were the ones that were in my dreams. I saw the symbols in my dreams before I read about them in the Word, which is how I made the connection and knew God was speaking. The intense and unique environment that I was subjected to during the dream was the clue that I needed to know that it was God speaking. In addition, the dreams would linger for days. I would relive the dream in the daytime, daydreaming. God's dreams are always positive, sometimes there are warnings but never fearful.

My dream experiences have altered slightly over the years. I can interact in the dream and I'm more aware that I am dreaming. Plus, as I said earlier, I now know when it is God speaking. I have a heightened sense of awareness and better recall. I can see clearer, and images are better defined. I look forward to my dreams, but I can't control when it happens. There are times when I want to hear from God in a dream, but it escapes me. There are other times when I am preoccupied, focused, and not expecting it and he delivers. But one thing is for sure,: dreams only manifest when I am spending time with him, in prayer, worship, and study, which appears to be a prerequisite.

Cognitive Dissonance

The term cognitive dissonance is used to describe the mental discomfort that results from holding two conflicting beliefs, values, or attitudes.

What I have learned is with a firm understanding of this discomfort, we can use it effectively to shed light on a person's true motivations. When a person is confronted with conflicting beliefs, he is compelled to work to resolve the issue. But because the beliefs are conflicting, he only has one of two choices: to remove one of the conflicting beliefs by realizing the belief is in error, or to develop an illogical excuse to justify the conflicting beliefs.

When you observe one using irrational excuses to justify a wrong, then this should trigger the awareness that he may be under the influence of cognitive dissonance. With this knowledge, you now know he is using an excuse to justify his desire to support a poor choice and relieve his consciousness. Let's apply this knowledge to a common situation and illuminate the real motive.

A narcotics dealer is confronted by a friend. The friend states, "You are killing people with your drug dealings. Most of the ones you are killing are young teenagers." This places the dealer in an immediate cognitive dissonance situation. He cannot remain in this state because his conscious reminds him that what he is doing is wrong. As I said earlier, he has only two choices: one is to stop dealing which will remove the conflict; or develop an irrational excuse. Most likely the latter is his choice.

Excuses like the following will ensue: "If I don't sell it, someone else will, I'm not forcing them to take it, or I have no choice, for this is the only thing I know how to do." All three excuses are irrational and by no means justify the action. However, what the irrational excuse tells us is the dealer knows he is wrong but chooses not to address his behavior. A valid excuse isn't available, for there are no excuses to justify harming people in that manner.

I chose this example because it is obvious. However, in life, we will be exposed to more subtle cognitive dissonance situations that a far more difficult to see, especially if you are not looking. Here is another example, a father needs to discipline his son for poor behavior, but he doesn't like to do it for his son whines. This puts the father in a state of cognitive dissonance. He knows without proper discipline, his son will suffer the consequences, and coupled with his non-action, we have a conflict. Again, he has two choices, discipline his son and the conflict is resolved, or stand behind an excuse. In this case, he makes up an excuse: "I'll discipline him the next time, boys will be boys, or I don't care what he does he is beyond hope."

Armed with our knowledge of cognitive dissonance, we can spot irrational excuses and can now allow the excuses to point to the real motivator, his dislike of disciplining his son and his weakness in acting.

Let's try an even more subtle conflict. A wife questions her husband when he stays out too late without calling home to let her know. The conflict he is not following the agreed-upon rule when staying out late. The proper result would be for the husband to admit his error and work to resolve the issue for the betterment of their relationship. Instead, the husband screams at his wife so she will drop the accusation. Or he may even walk out of the room, say something like, "You think you are perfect and do no wrong." Or even worse, he strikes her. All three acts are inappropriate and are the result of cognitive dissonance. Some may think this type of behavior is rare, but I assure you this is highly typical. With the understanding of cognitive dissonance, we now know the issue isn't that she brought up the problem but his lack of desire to confront his poor behavior.

Knowledge of cognitive dissonance has benefitted me greatly in a multitude of situations, prevented me from focusing on the wrong motives, and brought to light the reasons for irrational excuses and poor behavior. Also, this has helped me to shed light on some of my flaws. If you are anything like me, you will be shocked at how easy it is to create irrational excuses to hide behind.

The Absence Of Critical Thinking And The Lack Of Knowledge

The University of Louisville defines critical thinking as follows:

> Critical thinking is the intellectually disciplined process of actively and skillfully conceptualizing, applying, analyzing, synthesizing, and/or evaluating information gathered from, or generated by, observation, experience, reflection, reasoning, or communication, as a guide to belief and action.

Critical thinking is essential to combating the deceptions of the enemy. Without it, you are prey, easily manipulated to perform desired actions without your awareness. Couple the absence of critical thinking with the lack of knowledge, then we are like blind sheep, useful idiots to the enemy. I realized that was a harsh statement, but it is true, and it had to be stated. If it offended you and you stopped reading this book, there was no loss here for you have no desirable usefulness.

My people are destroyed for lack of knowledge. **Hosea 4:6 (KJV)**

Leave them; they are blind guides. If the blind lead the blind, both will fall into a pit. **Matthew 15:14 (NIV)**

A communist plan to take over a nation was discovered decades ago and numerous books in circulation illustrate the strategic plan of how it would have infiltrated the country from within and gradually convert it into a socialist nation. In America, this plan is being played out right before our eyes and many are unknowingly supporting the effort. Socialism has taken over numerous countries already, like China, Russia, Venezuela, North Korea, and Cuba to name a few. The process takes the lives of tens of millions. It is written in the history books, yet it continues to succeed in taking over countries. The results are mass death and a massive decrease in the standard of living. It includes the loss of liberty, personal rights, and living in an oppressive regime. The results of socialism aren't hidden from the public, they are there for the world to see.

The questions you must ask yourself are, how can a disease like communism spread across the face of the earth without adequate resistance to repel it? How can so many people be deceived by its takeover plan when it is well-documented? The answer to those questions is people lack critical thinking which leads to the failure to educate themselves. We seek to educate ourselves when we are aware of a deficiency that causes us harm.

Socialism has come out of hiding and is being pushed upon this nation. Every person with normal intellect is confronted with this knowledge. Now, a sheep will accept socialism as being good for them because the mass media has told them so. They will support it because they trust their leaders and the media. However, history is full of failed regimes that have oppressed, enslaved, killed, and banished their subjects. With that in mind, logic dictates we need to confirm socialism is either good or not good for this nation and ourselves. This is where critical thinking comes into play. Critical thinking immediately brings up these questions: where has communism been instituted before? What is life like under these regimes? Is communism better than what we currently have? What is the cost of the conversion to communism? The answer to each of those questions is unfavorable for communism. No one will support communism if they have done their research, unless they believe they will be in the ruling class. So, don't look to the likely ruling class for answers; for them, communism is favorable.

Next, critical thinking moves us to consider how a disease like communism can successfully take over a nation. Consequently, we are driven to educate ourselves about the takeover process which leads to the consumption of articles, books, and various other documentation. Now educated, we see the plans of communism in play all around us, in our elected government officials, our governmental departments, in the public school system, and in the media. Armed with the knowledge that socialism/communism is not desirable and the knowledge of their takeover plan, we can successfully defeat it.

Labeling People

This tactic of labeling people, groups, and individuals has been used for centuries to justify treating people inhumanely, and unjustly. It has led to prejudices, biases, and many types of other abuses. It has been used in a mastery fashion; during colonialism, the Europeans used it quite skillfully. When they engaged a people in a foreign land, they would quickly label them as uncivilized, barbaric, and even savages. Why? This allowed them to sever their consciousness from true reality, kill unmercifully and proceed inhumanely. Europeans lived under the banner of Christianity—killing and inhumane behavior were unacceptable. The labels provided a way around the decrees: killing animals, savages and beasts are not evil.

During the forgotten Indian Ocean slave trade of peoples of Africa, the Arabs enslaved African women and castrated the men. No one with a normal conscious could perform such horrific tasks on ordinary people. These acts were deemed acceptable because indigenous and African people were labeled less than human.

My purpose here is not to bring up history to make one feel guilty. I want to apply a jolt to your being so that what I'm going to bring up next will not be so easily dismissed.

Humanity is capable of some horrendous acts. We label people now as it was done in the past to justify abusing our own children, friends, neighbors, and family members. We justify not working with people groups to solve problems with easy solutions. We use it to divide and elevate ourselves unjustifiably. These labels could be mild, like "He's not too bright... bless her heart... she's blond... he is smart but lacks common sense... or he is selfish". When we apply these mild labels, we are justifying the poor actions or comments that follow.

An example: little Johnny is riding his bike down the street and accidentally stops too quickly with his front brakes and tumbles over the handlebars onto the pavement. The correct thing to do is to rush to his aid with compassion. Instead, we laugh and respond with a comment like, "He is so clumsy and stupid. It is a wonder he hasn't killed himself already." The clumsy and stupid label gives our conscious the excuse it needs to not act compassionately.

Harsher labels give us the excuse we need to act more egregiously. We can sexually assault a beautiful young woman, label her as an undocumented wetback and leave the scene of the crime with no sense of remorse. We can even justify it: "That's what she gets for coming into this country illegally."

What we must understand is that we are all made in the image of God and no label will ever change that. If we are smarter, prettier, wealthier, or more fortunate than another, consider it a blessing but it doesn't elevate our status. The more you have, the more is required of you. Consider that fact the next time you feel the need to label someone.

Children have different personalities: one kid finds it hard to follow parental rules if the need for the rule is not explained, while another will follow rules without any explanation. Neither kid is wrong, they are just wired differently. The parent of the first kid may label the kid as stubborn and treat him harshly and unjustly. The stubborn label prevented the parent from searching further for the child's need for an explanation. So, this child suffered a childhood of unjust behavior towards him because he was labeled stubborn. This situation is common and there are many more just like it.

I have heard parents label their kids as dumb, stupid, worthless, ignorant, etc. This breaks my heart. It is hard for me to keep my composure when I hear it, I literally want to smack them. How you can do this to a child is beyond me. This kills their self-esteem; it drives them to live up to that label.

Some of these labels have a lifetime effect on our children's personalities. We carelessly label them, giving little thought to their impact. As parents, we have an incredible influence on the outcome of our kids. This realization humbles me for I feel wholly inadequate to take on the task of fatherhood, what an enormous responsibility.

In the Hebrew language, names have meanings. If a person's name didn't characterize a person's true nature, God would change the person's name. Saul became Paul, Sara became Sarah, Abram became Abraham and Jacob became Israel. Their names were changed to encourage them to take on new Godly behaviors or discard poor behaviors. God used labels but he used them positively and correctly. So positive labels work to our advantage but negative labels work against us. However, positive labels must be true, or the label-barer' abilities will not match their label. Telling a poor public speaker that they are an excellent speaker may prevent him from seeking to improve himself.

Each political party labels the other as racist, morally bankrupt, and a lost cause. With the label firmly attached, the ability to work together is lost. When they participate in meetings, there isn't any mutual respect, the atmosphere is full of animosity, and the environment is caustic. There is no surprise that little fruit comes from these meetings and the bridge between the political parties widens. I have heard this statement from a politician, "If I find myself agreeing with the opposing party, I will reexamine my decision for it is probably wrong." There isn't much of a chance that this politician will work with the other side. Congress is made up of mature and well-educated people, yet they act in such a childlike manner, unaware of the consequences of labeling the other party so ruthlessly.

Here is an extremely clever tactic of our enemy, Satan and unfortunately, he uses some people unknowingly to accomplish it. He takes one political party and deceives them into thinking they are working for good. He labels their bad actions with good labels, but the results of their actions are in direct opposition to God. Their actions are destroying the very fabric of society. Satan knows that the results of the deceived party's actions will manifest in society and his deceit will be exposed. However, he is one step ahead and labels the other party as the ones who are destroying society. So, when society starts to erode, the wrong party gets blamed. It is a devious plot created by a mastermind. However, his plan is easily exposed: take a party's core beliefs and shine the light of God's Word on it. Not yours and society's desired outcome but the unadulterated Word of God. Remove the labels society has placed on their core beliefs and actions so you can see it as God intended it to be seen.

The need for some people to hold on to labels is great. If you have performed some egregious acts under the umbrella of a label, you must not abandon the label, or your previous acts will be exposed, and you will need to comfort them. For example, you labeled your child as dumb and stupid. Your child became that label. You later realized that your labeling led your child to that behavior. So, you must never admit that a child is not dumb or stupid; to do so would be admitting you were the cause. Or you are presently mistreating African Americans: you must hold onto the n-word, or you will have to stop your mistreatment.

As a society, we must refrain from putting labels on family members, people, and groups of people. We need to examine the labels we are currently using and discard them when they are not appropriate; the cost is too high not to.

God's Laws And Decrees

Society seems to fight against God's laws and decrees. To the world, the laws appear to be unnecessarily restrictive; they keep you from enjoying life to its fullest.

I was tutoring a young man in junior high, and the conversation came up about salvation. I asked him if he believed in God and was saved. His response was that he did believe in God, but he wasn't ready to be saved because there were many things he wanted to do, and being a Christian would hinder that. After drilling deeper, it wasn't any one thing he was concerned about, it was more of a general belief. This belief that being a Christian takes away from your freedom is a common misconception, for God's laws and decrees do the opposite. They are not arbitrary but designed to move us away from actions that are detrimental to us.

Consider this analogy: a driver has two routes he can take to get to his destination. There is a fork in the road, and each path leads to his destination, but he must travel through one of two cities. There are signs posted at the fork that describe the city's traffic laws.

The first route takes him through a city called "Law and Order" which has well-defined traffic laws. Its laws were designed to ensure vehicles are in good repair, drivers receive training to ensure they can drive safely, and police officers are out to enforce adherence to the laws. There are traffic lights, stop signs, speed limits, car inspections, driver's license requirements, etc. All the expected driver and traffic laws.

Alternatively, the second city, 'Freedom Ville', believes in total freedom, there are no restrictions. No traffic lights or signs, but you are told to proceed with caution, and when traveling through intersections, use your best judgment. There are no speed limits, so one can drive as fast as one likes but you are encouraged not to drive at an unsafe speed. No driver's license is required; however, please do not drive if you cannot drive safely. You can drive on either side of the road, for we need to accommodate our foreign drivers who are used to driving on the left side of the road. We are aware that some of our low-income drivers may have difficulty keeping their vehicles in good repair; therefore, safety inspections are voluntary. Finally, if you are involved in a traffic accident, the honor system applies. You only need to pay the percentage of the total cost of the repairs that is directly proportional to your contribution to the accident. In Freedom Ville, we believe that all people are responsible citizens, make good choices, and can be trusted to do what is right and just.

The analogy appears to be absurd, but isn't it true to what society is seeking? Freedom Ville was trying to please everyone and ended up pleasing no one. When foreigners come to America, they need to follow the laws set here. You can't have sets of contradictory laws any more than you can have both left and right-side road drivers. I understand there are financial difficulties, I have lived through them, but you can't compromise voting integrity any more than vehicle safety. You must find another way to solve the problem that will not negatively impact society. People can't be trusted to pay their fair share, there must be laws to enforce them. They will abuse the law, so licenses must be required, and speed limits enforced.

The first city, 'Law and Order' has many laws, but laws are necessary to keep a city safe and manageable. It will prevent people from suffering from making poor choices and from allowing irresponsible people to harm others. You have the freedom to go where you like and to get there safely. The second city appears to be freer for there are no restrictions but due to the lack of laws, the city is unsafe, and it is unlikely that you will get to your destination. If you live in that city, you will surely be at a high risk of having multiple accidents, body injuries, suffering loss due to vehicle damage, etc.

What is being demanded by society is as absurd as it is depicted by the analogy. The consequences are vastly more damaging, and the scope, worldwide.

The Belief In Self

The greatest commandment is to love God with all you have and the second is just like it, love your neighbor as yourself. You see, our society has moved self from the third position to the first position and has moved God to the third position. With self-being the highest priority, men seek to be self-reliant so in this way, they can remove God from the equation altogether.

The more complex a society is, the more dependent we are on others. I have heard people say they don't need anyone. Self-reliance is an illusion; it is one that Satan presents to the arrogant. The arrogant embrace it with pride and a deep sense of self-satisfaction. However, with a little critical thinking, this deception can be quickly dispelled.

First, let's consider God's contributions to our lives: all of creation, including the planet, food, water, shelter, our bodies, air to breathe, healing, a future, etc. Without God's contribution, there is no us. Second, farmers take seeds and plant them, cultivate the seeds, and harvest the plants with many hours of physical labor. The plants are then prepared and shipped to the stores for us to purchase. Consider what it takes to put animal protein on our plates, and produce automobiles, what it takes for education, our employers, the medical field, etc.

You see self-reliance is only an illusion. True self-reliance is impossible without God. And it is impossible without others. Even for the atheist who takes God out of the equation, self-reliance would appear to be something like this. You live on ten acres of land on an isolated island. That person would have to produce their food, clothes, and water supply. They will need to educate themselves (without books for that comes from someone else's work), provide shelter with only raw materials from their land, provide their own medical needs, and methods for traveling are just a few things for starters. Just those basic needs would require most of us to spend the bulk of our time surviving with very little time to do anything else. And we haven't addressed our desires that exceed our needs. A harsh winter, or extended drought, and most of us would die.

In the Bible, God uses the sheep as an animal representation of Israel and/or the church. As sheep, we need protection and a guide. This representation is used in many parables for I believe it is because of our need for a shepherd. We were designed that way. Goats are more independent than sheep and have less need for a shepherd. They are more adaptable than sheep for independent survival. When speaking of the world in Biblical parables, God usually refers to the ungodly as goats for they see no need for the Good Shepherd. However, with a good shepherd, the number of sheep survivors increases astronomically far more than the independent goats.

Other things to consider: when sheep and goats are herded together, the male goats are aggressive and dominate the herds. The sheep are passive and follow the shepherd more readily. Male goats have short straight horns while most male sheep are without horns. Male goats ram other goats; and sheep by standing on their hind legs at a 45-degree angle while launching forward toward their targets with great force. An un-horned male sheep is at a disadvantage. This is an excellent picture of the world and how the godly and ungodly interact with each other.

A good shepherd works to minimize the negative effect on the male goats. God raises a superior foe from time to time to combat the effects of the ungodly. Occasionally a male sheep will grow horns. A ram has much larger horns on the side of its head; they curve backward and are much larger than a goat's. Plus, the rams have superior tactics when fighting. The ram does not stand on his hind legs and launches forward but accelerates on all fours while remaining on the ground and strikes his target. This is another excellent picture of the godly. As mentioned earlier, in battle the goat stands on its hind legs with its chest elevated and exposed and launches towards its target. The ram, on the other hand, rams into the midsection of the goat while he is elevated. The goat either doesn't survive or is severely wounded. Unfortunately, horned male rams are scarce while all male goats are horned.

When we believe we are self-reliant we are like goats, we tend not to depend on the Good Shepherd as we should. We look to ourselves for the provision and the answers to life. We see others around us achieving success and believe they are self-made. With the illusion of self-made successes all around us, we embrace their teachings and methods--we seek to mimic them. When goats are leading, all success is worldly because goats don't know what is important. However, the sheep's shepherd knows what is best and leads the sheep into success that they could never conceive of. While the godly know that the beginning of wisdom is the fear of the Lord. Worldly success is valueless. What would it benefit a man if he gained the whole world and lost his very soul?

What is greater, a homeless gentleman of poor health that struggled with substance addiction his whole life due to a great number of mistakes, but he loves the Lord? Or a youthful, healthy, worldly self-made multi-billionaire who has no perceived need for a savior?

Also, when we are self-reliant, we look inward to our own thinking for answers to life-critical questions. Consider this analogy: let's say you have the power to create, and you created one hundred widgets. You gave the widget life. Let's assume you are of sufficient intellect and just did not create a life for the fun of it, but you had a purpose. Now, should the newly created widgets look to you for their purpose or seek their purpose within themselves? The answer to that question is obvious. Yet so many of us search for the answer to life in the wrong place. Your relationship with your creator should be the most important. And the good of society should be placed above your own for the creator created many, not one. All of life should be seen from that prism: the creator first, society, and then yourself.

Do Not Judge

Do not judge, or you too will be judged. For in the same way you judge others, you will be judged, and with the measure you use, it will be measured to you. Why do you look at the speck of sawdust in your brother's eye and pay no attention to the plank in your own eye? How can you say to your brother, 'Let me take the speck out of your eye,' when all the time there is a plank in your own eye? You hypocrite, first take the plank out of your own eye, and then you will see clearly to remove the speck from your brother's eye. **Matthew 7:1-5**

God isn't speaking to the upright Christian, he is speaking to the hypocrite, one that does not walk the Godly path and is quick to judge others. I emphasize this because I have heard the use of these verses to justify telling true Christians not to judge sin when they are witnesses to it, for the Christian to turn a blind eye to it. God tells true Christians to judge them by their fruit.

We must read the Word in context; he is speaking to the hypocrites as clearly stated in verse five. Those who confess Christ, but do not follow him. Those who judge in this way, God judges them with the same measure that they pour out on others. As a result of the hypocritical judgment of others and subsequent judgment from God, their lives are full of trials and tribulations. Life seems to be more difficult for them than what is endured by their peers. Especially those that supply judgment unmercifully. Peace seems to escape them; success seems to be momentary. The characteristic of a highly judgmental person is that he fails to find joy. He may find temporary worldly success, but he will fail to find the joy that Christ gives that surpasses all understanding. Judgmental people tend to flock together and feed off each other.

God says to the hypocrite, "Remove the stick from your eye so you can see clearly to remove the speck from your brothers." So, he says to help remove the speck from your brother's eye but to take care of their home first. To cease judging until your home is right--in other words, be doers of the Word not just speakers of the Word.

They See Without Seeing And Hear Without Hearing (Part 1)

And the disciples came, and said unto him, Why speakest thou unto them in parables?
He answered and said unto them, Because it is given unto you to know the mysteries of the kingdom of heaven, but to them, it is not given.
For whosoever hath, to him shall be given, and he shall have more abundance: but whosoever hath not, from him shall be taken away even that he hath.
Therefore speak I to them in parables: ***because they seeing see not, and hearing they hear not, neither do they understand. Matthew 13:10-13 (KJV)***

How is it possible that normal, healthy individuals are unable to see or hear when their senses are functioning normally? The data received by the senses does enter their brains, but its influence appears to be lost. It seems impossible at first glance. The reason for this situation is we all have an internal filter that interrogates information received from the senses. This filter operates between our consciousness and our senses.

The filter eliminates what is deemed unimportant, false, irrelevant, or incomprehensible. Otherwise, our minds would be full of meaningless information. In the case of the parables, the parables couldn't be understood so what was spoken was dispensed.

Jesus stated, "Because it is given unto you to know the mysteries of the kingdom of heaven, but to them, it is not given." They will see without seeing and hear without understanding. When we commit to Christ, our hearts are changed; or in other words, our filter is altered so we begin to see like God sees and hear as God hears.

This makes a great deal of sense, for the parables were about the hidden kingdom. The parables require you to believe in the kingdom as a prerequisite, which sequentially allows the parable to pass through our filter.

Two men are in a densely populated wooded area. A partial moon is out but very little light is available. One man says to the other, "We do not know how much farther it is to our destination, we are unable to see clearly where we are stepping. In addition, I hear the aggressive sounds of wild animals that I cannot see, I know the animals are close by, and we have no reference point to guide us. I strongly suggest that we return the way we came, back to safety, the risk is just too great."

The other man disagrees with that assessment and says, "I'm positive we can reach our destination."

They could not agree, so they parted ways. The first man found his way back to safety, the other was never heard of again.

What is the meaning of this little adventure? Is the story worth retaining? This story is like a parable: you hear it, but its meaning escapes you, unless you had foreknowledge of an event like this that is foreseeable and knew to expect it. What if you had a personal relationship with God and God revealed vital information to you long before you were exposed to the little adventure?

"The path to the Kingdom will be hidden to the non-believer, but I will tell you what to expect. Trust in me, I will walk beside you and lead you through the difficult trails to your destination. Do not despair."

With the foreknowledge revealed by God, the little story has a great hidden meaning. You must trust in God if you intend to reach the kingdom. He will guide you, and you can't discover the way without him. You might have to travel by yourself; your trusted human companion may not be up for the challenge and the world may be unaware that you reached your destination.

Without the revelation, the story is valueless and meaningless. Your internal filter will discard the parable. With the revelation, however, treasures are revealed. This is how it is with parables.

We can also fail to hear and see things in our everyday lives due to who we align ourselves with, and who we believe and trust. Our adversary is cunning and brilliant, and he always has a well-developed plan. Deception is his main tool, and he doesn't reveal his overall strategy but to a few; you must be aware of his schemes in advance to avoid falling prey to them. He distributes instructions and knowledge compartmentally, so most don't know the larger strategy. Consequently, the devil uses people unknowingly, but top leaders are typically aware. The devil leads a third of the angels as well as human leaders, some knowingly, some unknowingly.

This group that Satan leads has integrated itself into world leadership, and governments. Unfortunately, people so readily believe and trust in the government. Governments can be led by God; this is what God desired. The government was designed to be used by God as a tool to govern men; unfortunately, we handed it over to Satan. Now, when we commit to governments, we commit to Satan. Most will never admit it for they don't believe that is a true statement, but it is true. Let me demonstrate how beholding we are to the government. Let's say there is a group of thirty houses set on ten acres of land. If for some reason their food supply was cut, they would solicit the government for food and maybe even suffer from starvation. However, growing crops on the ten acres of land and becoming self-sufficient would not be in their immediate sphere. Able-body adults would look to the government before themselves.

When it comes to changing our society, who do we trust to get this accomplished—the government, not God? Do we not blame our problems on the other political party of said government? This indirectly points to the belief that the other party can affect society, so we blame our ills on them. If the other political party is the blame for our ills, then you must admit that the government is in control, therefore it is your God.

I submit that ultimately it isn't the government that is your God, but Satan and the spirits that follow him.

> *For we wrestle not against flesh and blood, but against principalities, against powers, against the rulers of the darkness of this world, against spiritual wickedness in high places.* **Ephesians 6:12 (KJV)**

So, when we seek after the government to solve our problems, we are seeking after Satan.

One strategy that Satan uses is to give us a few non-consequential things that we desire, then he gets us to commit to him and with that commitment, he leads us to destruction.

My mother said, "When I was a little girl, I would have to kill chickens to prepare them to be dinner." She would hold out her hand with feed and the chicken would approach her for the treat, she would then grab the chicken and wring its neck. Now chickens are not smart and a chicken that just watched his fellow chicken get his neck wring, would approach my mother for a treat as well. Don't laugh, for we, the church, do the same. Satan uses this same strategy with us: our governmental leaders give us programs that benefit us, but at the same time, they institute policies that destroy the very fabric of society. We see without seeing and we hear without hearing. Free steak dinner with slow-killing poison is not a dinner I want to eat.

If you have a dog that lives outside and twice a day you leave food for him to eat, he is rarely home but always ventures back to the house at the expected mealtime. With the trust you have built in the dog, you can easily destroy him in many ways: poison his meals, put up physical traps around the food bowl, have a different color dog take his food from him when he is halfway through it, switch the food stealing dogs periodically, but ensure each is the same color. This will cause the dog to hate the other colored dogs, for sees them as the ones taking his food. There are dozens of things that can be done to manipulate the dog and force a particular behavior. We can put a shock collar on the dog that is triggered when he howls or barks, taking away his ability to communicate with other dogs. We can put prey in the yard, if he attempts to subdue the prey, we take away his meal. Devious isn't it, but governments do it all the time.

Everyone can see a completely depraved group of people that have no good in them. It is the wolf in sheep's clothing that is hard to distinguish. The question is, how does one distinguish between groups whose intentions are ultimately bad but hide them with gifts from other groups with good intentions but fail occasionally due to the flaws of their humanity? Both groups can appear the same, but wisdom distinguishes them. The deceivers are murderers. They fight against God's foundational truths like family and harming the innocent. They corrupt standards that God has set; what God has made beautiful.

Followers of the God-hating group will make the beautiful, profane. Like music: God's followers will make beautiful music. If not Christian music, it will still be of good quality. Those who hate God will have music laced with profanity, and boast about things that God hates like greed, sexual perversion, and rants of derogatory attacks at the expense of others. They and their followers do these things.

In their art, God lovers will produce paintings of God's handiwork like paintings of sunsets, landscapes, people, etc. Sculptures that are not deformed or ugly. Haters of God produce abstract art, art that has no value but is hidden in a lie. Deformed sculptures, the ugly.

As said earlier, when we become saved, we are given a new heart, and to a limited extent, we see and hear as God does. Remember, God says, "Only those that do the will of the Father will enter into the kingdom of Heaven," (Matthew 7:21-23) and consequently are saved. Only doers of the Word see the perversions done to the works of God and they hate it, while the non-doers label it beautiful.

Another reason why some see without seeing and hear without hearing is when one is communicating with another and there isn't a common point of reference. Let's consider a blind man born blind and the same with a deaf man born deaf. If you attempted to describe the rainbow with all its colors to the blind man, it would be impossible for there is no common point of reference, no visual experience to which the blind man could appeal. This would be true for the deaf man as well. If you attempted to describe a symphony to him, it would be impossible for him to understand.

When one believes in his own abilities and that he is too clever to be deceived, this individual has a filter that protects his consciousness and does not allow any data that contradicts his worldview to reach his mind and be evaluated. He too would be blind to the truth if he didn't already have it.

Consider this scenario, one gave his life to Christ, and he is convinced he is saved. However, Christ never penetrated his heart. This is evident in his lack of knowing and following the will of God in his life. In this state, he falsely believes that he is saved. Now couple that with his belief that he is too wise to succumb to deception, so his filter filters out all that is contradictory to his own beliefs. Since his heart hasn't changed, he doesn't see and hear like the Father and therefore he filters out the truth.

This state of mind is summed up quite nicely in **Jeremiah 17:9**

> *The heart is deceitful above all things, and desperately wicked: who can know it? (KJV)*

Here is a fruitless habit that we must overcome, but it is extremely difficult to do, and that is attempting to convince a person that can't see to see. We described the object, and we used sound logic and reasoning hoping for a breakthrough, but there was no progress. Next, we get angry with the person for not seeing, and then we begin to question their intellect and or sanity. I believe the right approach here is to ask God to open their eyes, to remove the blinders. At the same time, we should also ask God to remove any blinders or deceptions from our eyes. Remember we are deceivable, whenever we think we are not. At that moment we become deceivable.

I was once an Atheist, and my beliefs were absolute. If I had a billion dollars at that time in my life, I would have easily and without hesitation bet it all on the fact there wasn't a God. Consequently, if I had passed away during this time, I would have been the most surprised person in hell. I had a filter in that state of my life that when I was confronted by someone speaking of God, I considered it foolishness and filtered it out, discarded it. This is the same way the deceived responds to truth: they filter it out and discard it. I was not seeing and hearing the truth. As a blind man can't perceive colors or a deaf person can't appreciate music, it is all the same.

However, all things work for good for those who love Christ. An ex-drug user's testimony can help a current user through his addiction, and an ex-alcoholic can witness to a drunker. Therefore, I can witness to the deceived for I have been there.

It is extremely embarrassing to be called by God a fool, but I mention it so I will remain humble and never forget where he brought me from. Can I be deceived? Yes, yes, yes. With that in mind, I continuously check and recheck my beliefs against the Word. It must be anchored in the truth; if not, it can most definitely be wrong. I will listen to anyone but if you desire for me to believe in your viewpoints, you support it with God's Word, or I will only consider it an opinion. Like the deceived who has a filter, I have one too--it is the Word of God.

I thank God for going through the transition from atheist to Christian, from fool to wisdom. Those who haven't experienced a life-altering deception do not have the point of reference that I have. Not that they haven't succumbed to deception; no, they are just not aware of it and cannot conceive that it is possible.

This makes them ripe for deception. When a person thinks he can't be deceived, then he is the embodiment of deception. I It is where deception lives. He relies on his thinking, easily manipulated by Satan.

Remember these words from God.

> *Wherefore by their fruits ye shall know them.*
> *Not everyone that saith unto me, Lord, Lord, shall enter into the kingdom of heaven; but he that doeth the will of my Father which is in heaven.*
> *Many will say to me in that day, Lord, Lord, have we not prophesied in thy name? and in thy name have cast out devils? and in thy name done many wonderful works?*
> *And then will I profess unto them, I never knew you: depart from me, ye that work iniquity.*
> **Matthew 7:20-23 (KJV)**

Noticed that the deceived responded with their experiences of miracles committed on their watch as if that cemented their salvation. God responded, "Depart from me, I do not know you."

Fortunately, God gives us a method of proof to gauge our Christian walk: we must be doing the will of God. So, we must ask ourselves, what is God's will in our lives? What has he called us to do? Am I currently doing his will?

Second, Jesus says to those who were deceived, "I do not know you." So, do you have a personal relationship with God? If you can't answer these questions with a resounding yes, then you are not ready to stand before the Lord. It is that simple. If you say you are ready but can't answer yes to the above questions laid out here, you are deceiving yourself.

What does it mean to have a relationship with God? This can't be described fully in words; it must be experienced. During prayer, worship, or just plain existence, God is there. Peace, joy, understanding, love, and security are there as well. Holiness, righteousness, awe, and power are spiritually sensed when you are in his presents, and you can only praise him. The praise doesn't come from what you know of God in an external sense but from what you know of Him when you are submerged in His presence. All you need and desire is there. You lack wanting, and you are fully satisfied. Full disclosure of who I am, fully exposed but fully accepted. You are with God. This state is only a shallow of what it will be when we are in His presence in our immortal bodies.

God walks with us through life, leads and guides as we travel together. He communicates with us constantly.

Solomon was the wisest man ever, but he staggered away from God and followed paganism. He was deceived into thinking that it was possible to find value outside of God. Once he realized his flaw, he returned to God. So, if the wisest man can be deceived, surely we can. Solomon checked himself, we should do the same before we hear these words, "Depart from me, I do not know you."

Another thing to keep in mind: some non-Christians live better lives than Christians; they live by the laws written on their hearts, but they don't know God personally. Satan knows of God, but he doesn't follow God, he is one who truly knows God and follows his commandments.

He that saith, I know him, and keepeth, not his commandments, is a liar, and the truth is not in him.
1 John 2:4 (KJV)

They See Without Seeing And Hear Without Hearing (Part 2)

When the Bible refers to the heart, it is believed that it is speaking of the subconscious. The conscious mind is where we interact with the world, the subconscious is where our worldview lives. It is the holder of our value system, our motivator, and the why that drives us to act. The conscious and subconscious are not always in agreement. Therefore, an individual can be a living contradiction.

An example of this is when one confesses that he loves God, knows his commandments, and studies the Word but produces no spiritual fruit. The conscious mind made the decision to follow Christ, but the subconscious was hardened and never accepted Christ. As indicated in part one of this section, there is a filter that allows the conscious not to absorb data when it believes it is valueless. For the subconscious, the heart can prevent inputs from penetrating it. This is referred to as the hardening of one's heart. The heart is hardened by poor behaviors like unconfessed sin, harsh judgment, anger, and unforgiveness. In the conscious mind, we deal with things as long as they are in our memory.

These people honor me with their lips, but their hearts are far from me. **Matthew 15:8 (NIV)**

You see, man can easily speak righteously, and his heart is as hard as a stone, far from God.

I was working with a ministry which worked with drug addicts and the homeless. We were gathered in a small church and preparing to begin worship. A young man whom I saw for the first time was speaking to another gentleman. This young man was quoting scriptures and speaking as one with a strong relationship with God.

Later that day, he asked me if I was cursed, and I quickly responded no. I wondered why he asked me that question, but I didn't probe. Once service was over, the group gathered outside and socialized. While we were conversing, the young man walked around the perimeter of the group and started cursing the group. I initially was going to confront him, but I felt in my spirit this wasn't the right thing to do. So, I prayed fervently against what he was saying. No one noticed what the young man was doing but me. Anyway, he quickly ceased cursing and looked puzzled. I'm not sure what happened, but it was all God.

This got me thinking: how can someone quote scripture in that manner and then seek to curse another? Maybe there was a demon present, but I'm not sure. We can say this with absolute certainty: we are capable of extreme contradictions.

There have been numerous occasions where I have had a profound conversation with individuals and with the help of the Holy Spirit, this conversation has resulted in new Biblical revelations, a profound revelation that is an epiphany. This epiphany, when fully accepted in the heart, would create major life-altering changes. However, after the epiphany was accepted a few weeks later, the epiphany was abandoned, the old beliefs replaced it, and the impact of the epiphany was minimal to no effect.

Why? Although the conscious mind accepted it, the heart was hard and wasn't penetrated. Their value system never changed. Technically the old beliefs didn't return and replace the new. The epiphany only existed in the conscious mind, and once it failed to hold any significant time in memory, it faded out of existence.

Therefore, the scripture adamantly tells us to confess our sins daily, to forgive so we can be forgiven, to love our enemies, to avoid pride, not judge hypocritically, and to control our anger. If we fail to do any of these things, we severely hamper our Christian walk.

For example, there is an individual we dislike greatly. When the very mention of this person's name comes, a harsh feeling is stirred up in our hearts. This is an indicator that we are in a state of unforgiveness and living with hardened hearts. This is one of Satan's elaborate schemes to produce a mega villain which subsequently creates hatred against the villain and allows the hatred to harden hearts. If the mega villain doesn't repent and ends up in hell, then he will take the haters with him. If you can't forgive him and pray for him, you very well may see him on the other side of the pit. This lack of forgiveness may be the very reason why you are not producing fruit; you know that you should be producing fruit but fail to produce it. The way through this dilemma is to pray fervently for your enemies and love them.

I was watching a video program where a prisoner had requested to speak with the mother of the woman he raped and murdered. This scheduled meeting occurred over a video conference. The prisoner was on the screen in prison and the mother was attending as well as others. The prisoner had received a life sentence for his crime. He pleaded with the mother to forgive him; he had received Jesus while he was in prison and greatly regretted what he had done. He was earnest in his request.

"If it was possible," he stated, "I would give my life for your daughter." He said to the mother that he was not seeking to get out of prison, he was right where he belonged. All he asked for was the mother's forgiveness.

The mother responded and said, "You took my daughter from me, and I will never forgive you, never."

That was one of the moments when the Holy Spirit immediately grabbed my attention. The prisoner is in good standing with the Lord and if he died that day, he would have been with the Lord. His sins were forgiven by God. For the mother, the scriptures say, if you do not forgive those who sin against you, I will not forgive your sins. **Matthew 6:14-15.**

> *For if ye forgive men their trespasses, your heavenly*
> *Father will also forgive you:*
> *But if ye forgive not men their trespasses, neither will*
> *your Father forgive your trespasses.(KJV)*

Per God's words, she isn't forgiven and is under judgment. I bring to the light that forgiveness is not for the one who harmed you, forgiveness is for you. Without it, there is no hope. Don't be deceived and allow an evildoer, a Satan-produced villain, to lead you to have a hardened heart and miss out on God's blessings and even salvation.

They See Without Seeing And Hear Without Hearing (Part 3)

We talked about the filters for the conscious and subconscious mind in parts 1 and 2. Our conscious mind controls what the mouth speaks, the conscious can be used to restrict what is spoken from the heart. If one is secure enough, this would be seldom used to filter what comes out of the heart. Unless the heart is full of the unappealing and therefore concealment is desired. If one is full of hatred, anger, racism, and superiority, then what in the heart's voice will need to be contained around the general public? However, under extreme stress, this contained heart will speak directly through the tongue. Due to the stress, a decision is made to not control the tongue and let the heart speak. You can see this sometimes when someone is engaged in a verbal fight: they will say harsh things that are not typical in normal conversation. They later regret what they have spoken for the conscious mind is re-engaged and then must deal with the repercussions. However, rarely is the heart changed. This will become evident when the heart speaks in the same manner in the future. Exposure to the heart of this type, especially if it is a loved one, can be very disconcerting. Nevertheless, what is spoken from the heart should not be easily dismissed.

A good man brings good things out of the good stored up in his heart, and an evil man brings evil things out of the evil stored up in his heart. For the mouth speaks what the heart is full of. Luke 6:45 (NIV)

On the positive side of things, when we pray, we should pray from the heart.

*"When you seek me with all your **heart**, you will find me with you." **Jeremiah 29:13-14 (NIV)***

Without a doubt, we pray differently when we pray from the heart. Those heartfelt prayers can't be hindered by the conscious mind, we must allow the heart to speak unabatedly. Therefore, we should not pollute the heart with evil for the Holy Spirit can't speak through it. So, when you hear the heart of another speak with the fire of the Holy Spirit, you know what's in that heart. No one has a perfect heart that is devoid of evil, but the goal should be to minimize it to the point it doesn't hinder the Holy Spirit from speaking. Not just in prayer—the Holy Spirit speaks, but also in everyday conversation. It is the comforter, encourager, pointer to Jesus, bearer of the truth, peacekeeper, lover, forgiver, and dispenser of joy.

Take heed to what the heart (your heart and others) is speaking; otherwise, you will see without seeing and hear without hearing. The scripture says to judge them by their fruit. The heart speaks of the fruit within.

The scripture says in **Matthew 7:17-20:**

A good tree produces good fruit, and a bad tree produces bad fruit. A good tree can't produce bad fruit, and a bad tree can't produce good fruit. So every tree that does not produce good fruit is chopped down and thrown into the fire. Yes, just as you can identify a tree by its fruit, so you can identify people by their actions. (NLT)

When an evil heart speaks, it is producing bad fruit. Per the scripture, it cannot produce good fruit. Some may be asking themselves; some leaders produce good and bad fruit. This is an illusion, deception. The good is only provided to conceal the evil. Their ultimate goal is evil. A birthday cake with hidden rat poison appears to be good, but its ultimate goal is evil. Remember, one with a good heart only produces good. No evil is used to hide the good.

Progressive Morality

How can Christians both support and object to the same truth? Some Christians believe God's laws and decrees do not vary, while other Christians believe laws and decrees need to progress as society progresses. Alternatively stated in this manner, people change, and our laws need to adjust to the new way people think.

Society is a product of man, and it changes in the direction that men drive it. This is called progressive morality or just plain 'progressive.' Naturally, one must ask the next logical question: is God's Word static or dynamically driven by men in their control of society?

Jesus says,

> Do not think that I have come to abolish the Law or the Prophets; I have not come to abolish them but to fulfill them. For truly I tell you, until heaven and earth disappear, not the smallest letter, not the least stroke of a pen, will by any means disappear from the Law until everything is accomplished. Therefore anyone who sets

aside one of the least of these commands and teaches others accordingly will be called least in the kingdom of heaven, but whoever practices and teaches these commands will be called great in the kingdom of heaven. **Matthew 5:17-20 (NIV)**

This progressive society or group is not working for God. The opposite is true. Jesus says some will come in his name, so we expect an individual who says he is Jesus. This counterfeit Jesus will appear at some point in time, but this scenario isn't the only means someone can come as Jesus. A group can be the bearer of moral truth, convince the world that their moral truth is righteousness, and therefore replace God's moral truth. This is the spirit of the antichrist. They are wolves in sheep's clothing. So, it can be a single physical being posing as Jesus or a system of counter-moral truths posing as God's truths—both are antichrists.

Think of the most controversial laws that we have in the books now. At one time in the past, breaking those laws was illegal and carried a heavy penalty. Now those same acts are lawful and, in some cases, even encouraged. No doubt, men have changed, and society has changed as well. The ultimate question is, has God changed? Can what was once evil be good now? Is that possible?

Let's put our critical-thinking hats on now. If laws are progressive, our current laws are temporary and therefore what is wrong today will eventually be normal later. So eventually all evil acts will be acceptable in the future.

God was not blind-sided or not prepared for societal changes; He was well aware. This is verified by His prophets as they prophesy, which is detailed in the Word. God makes no provision for a morally changing society and no progressive laws. Why not prepare for a morally changing society? The answer to this is elementary: there is no such thing as a morally changing society, it is a society that deviates from set morality, and the only morality that counts is God's never-changing morality.

One clever way that society circumvents God's laws is by stating 'God is love.' I have heard this positive statement used too many times to justify sin. It is treated as if God's love for man keeps Him from judging mankind and forces Him to accept sin. His love leaves Him powerless to judge. It is used to nullify all laws and decrees. Love isn't the only thing God is: He is righteous, holy, all-powerful, omnipresent, just, and don't forget, judge. JUDGE, meaning if you want to know what standards you need to follow, you use the standards that the judge will use.

What if God says horses are not to mate until they are married, and once they are married, they can only mate with each other? Mating outside of marriage is a slippery slope that leads to a bottomless pit. So, the two horses are friends but are not married and they are leisurely walking and fellowshipping. They see the path that God told them not to travel, a path to the mating. We can't say because they are great friends who love each other, they should be allowed to travel the forbidden path. How can so many people miss seeing the logical flaw in that statement? Traveling the path and friendship are mutually exclusive. You do not need to mate with someone to love them. Some say, because God is love, the forbidden path shouldn't be denied to friends. A loving God would not deny it. This is due to their short-sightedness. That path leads to the destruction of the family, and the results are around us.

Progressive morality also believes we should remove God's laws from our governmental laws as if that makes God's laws no longer valid. That is foolishness, the separation between Church and State. Governmental officials and politicians openly say that they will not let their Biblical views affect how they govern. God's laws are designed for everyone, everywhere, and all the time.

When one says he will not allow his Biblical views to affect him while he is governing, the removal of his Biblical views does not leave a vacuum, it's filled with someone's laws. If God's laws are not followed when governing, whose laws are to be followed? Is it men's progressive laws? Anyone with a little knowledge of history would shudder at that prospect happening. Genocide, racism, slavery, oppression, child sacrifice, child trafficking, unjustified wars, etc. If I listed all the atrocities committed by governments, you wouldn't have had the time to read this book. Also, I'm not speaking about the past, it is still actively going on.

All Sin Is The Same?

"All sin is the same" is a statement I have heard numerous times, and it is untrue. Sometimes stated, "Sin is sin." The purpose of this statement is to justify doing or supporting an egregious sin by then comparing it to a lesser sin to remove its severity as if to make the two sins equal.

In the book of Numbers chapter 35, God spoke of different transgressions and the penalty for each. Their penalties were not the same, so this "all sin is the same" statement is a worldly statement, not Biblically based.

God has called out twenty-three sins, and if you practice these sins, you will not inherit the kingdom of God. These twenty-three sins are listed in the following verses:

I Corinthians 6:9-10
Galatians 5:19-20
Ephesians 5:5

Jesus spoke to the crowd, and they wanted to know who would be the greatest in the kingdom. He stated, "It is better that you tie a millstone around your neck and be thrown into the sea than to cause one of these little ones to stumble." Matthew 18:6) When perpetrating a sin against the innocent, it requires greater judgment.

God didn't destroy a nation due to oppression, slavery, racism, etc., but nations that spilled innocent blood were destroyed. That wasn't the only reason God destroyed nations, remember Sodom and Gomorrah. The Word tells us to not be deceived, those that commit these sins will not enter the kingdom of heaven. So, sins that prevent one from entering the Kingdom are greater due to the judgment allotted. So, all sin is not the same.

What baffles me are Christians who condone these so-called special sins that exclude one from heaven. Some may not agree with the sins, but they support those that do. What can the world offer one that would allow you to support what God hates, acts that require the greatest penalty of all, the exclusion from the kingdom? Do they not fear God? Do they not care about the ones that follow these sins, knowing they will perish? This is the highest level of cognitive dissonance. Society is the bread; these sins are the leaven. As the leaven spreads, more and more are populating hell. Extreme, cognitive dissonance is when you can hire someone that you know will put poison in your friend's birthday cake, but you can rationalize it as being acceptable by stating, "It is not I who put the poison in it."

However, "all sin is the same" does apply when it comes to the cross, for all sin required the blood of Jesus to be erased from our judgment. So, you can be forgiven for any of them. Simply repent of the sin, stop practicing the sin, and the blood of Jesus has cleansed you. Alternatively, don't repent and keep practicing the sin and the kingdom is off limits.

Personality Types

There are sixteen different personality types per Myers & Briggs. Each personality type has one of two subsets, assertive and turbulent. This gives you a total of thirty-two personality types. No one personality type is superior to another, all are essential to a healthy society. However, these personality types are not distributed equally throughout society. This is the work of the Creator. Specific personalities are better suited to function in particular positions such as leadership, advocacy, encouragement, science, etc. They are distributed in the right proportions for society to function such as there are far more followers than leaders. The personalities with the greater number will be more suited for a broader range of opportunities, while the rarer personality type, the more limited suitable opportunities.

If we function outside of what our personality fits, then we will not function at our best and likely be unsatisfied. With that in mind, I believe it is essential to know what personality type you are and what functions you are suited for. We all have free will; however, I believe the Creator has assigned special tasks for each of us. Our personality drives us in the direction He has planned for us. For example, one suited for solitary research will not be drawn to be a police officer or a public servant and will not be hidden away in an isolated campsite.

The more numerous your personality type, the easier it is for society to understand you. However, the rarer your personality, the more difficult it will be to be understood. Couple a rare personality with a minority race and a commitment to God, then you may never be understood. I express this scenario because it is the very condition I am in. For me, I have the rarest of the thirty-two types, .02% of the USA population. Compensate for race and being a Christian and you have .00065%. That is approximately one per 150,000 people.

When I read the description of my personality, it fits me perfectly. If I have free will, how can I be so predictable, how can we all be so predictable? I have reviewed other personality types, and their behaviors are just as predictable. When I was younger, I wanted to alter my personality because I didn't care for some of my traits. I tried but miserably failed, so I now wonder if it is possible. I am who God created me to be. If you don't like it, then you need to take that up with the Creator.

So many times, have I heard people suggest to others to take up behaviors like theirs, an introvert to be more extroverted, an empath to be less sensitive, a feeler to be more analytical, or a follower to lead. This comes from arrogance, to feel one's personality is correct, and others need to be changed.

I have been told that I am distant and unfriendly. Do you know why I appear that way? I'm distant and some consider that to be an unfriendly trait. People with my personality only have a few friends; their relationships are far more entrenched than average and require a greater level of trust and intimacy and a far greater commitment. This level of friendship is a must-have, and due to the commitment, there can only be a few. So, if you want to enter into a relationship with someone of that type, be willing to put in the work. If you violate their trust, it is almost impossible to get it back. This is why they are stand-offish, for their friendship bubble is closed off to casual relationships. It is not what they are looking for. What do I mean by that? Say you wanted a casual relationship with someone with my personality type, so you initiate a conversation and suggest that you call each other occasionally to stay in touch. That will likely not happen for we do not need a shallow relationship. However, if you suggested a weekly Bible study with targeted goals and objectives, this is much more likely. Within the weekly Bible study, a meaningful long-lasting relationship could flourish.

Why is all this important? It better defines your expectations. If you are aware of your rarity, then not being understood shouldn't cause you abnormal stress. You will be abnormal, but you will have a unique perspective. Use the gifts God gave you to accomplish His will. Your relationship with Him must be strong for He understands you; He created you.

For those on the other side of the spectrum and who have a common personality type, it is easy for you to see yourself as part of the masses, just one of many. Remember, Jesus said:

Enter through the narrow gate. For wide is the gate and broad is the road that leads to destruction, and many enter through it. But small is the gate and narrow the road that leads to life, and only a few find it." **Matthew 7:13-14 (NIV)**

Just because you can relate to most people, doesn't mean you should behave as they do. This is important because if you are following the crowd, then you are on the wrong path. Your walk with Christ should separate you. If it doesn't, then maybe it is time for a self-evaluation.

Having The
Right Perspective

Most of us perceive reality from a narrow perspective and therefore focus our attention on what is directly affecting us. Due to that perspective, we miss seeing the broader picture and therefore we don't target the right source of the issue. Fortunately, the Bible gives us the exact perspective to embrace.

Put on the full armor of God so that you can take your stand against the devil's schemes. For our struggle is not against flesh and blood, but against the rulers, against the authorities, against the powers of this dark world and against the spiritual forces of evil in the heavenly realms. Therefore put on the full armor of God, so that when the day of evil comes, you may be able to stand your ground, and after you have done everything, to stand. Stand firm then, with the belt of truth buckled around your waist, with the breastplate of righteousness in place, and with your feet fitted with the readiness that comes from the gospel of peace. In addition to all this, take up the shield of faith, with which you can extinguish all the flaming arrows of the evil one. Take the helmet of salvation and the sword of the Spirit, which is the word of God. and pray in the Spirit on all occasions with all kinds of prayers and requests. With this in mind, be alert and always keep on praying for all the Lord's people. **Ephesians 6:11-18 (NIV)**

These eight verses are packed full of information. They identify who our enemy is, his direct subordinates, their realms of authority, how to prepare for battle, their influence, what to expect, etc. The devil's battle plans are laid out throughout the Bible. He tries to topple God's plans, and he emulates God whenever he gets the opportunity. Satan hates humanity, and his goal is to kill, steal, and destroy as many as possible. Considering this knowledge, let's address each verse individually and then collectively.

Verse 11, *Put on the full armor of God so that you can take your stand against the devil's schemes.*

From this verse, we can determine we are in a battle, and we need to have armor to defend ourselves. Our enemy is the devil himself and he is using schemes to attack us. So, we need to be aware of his schemes. The issue here is we are not fully aware of the complexity, influence, broad range, and effectiveness of Satan's deceptions. This is in a general sense. I can't stress enough the need to know his schemes. I said in the chapter on logic and reasoning that a course needed to be taught to all students concerning logic at an early age, I believe this is true for the schemes of Satan as well.

From a specific sense, we are unaware of the devil's deceits as it applies to each of us individually. Consequently, we, the church, are losing the battle.

There are ways to determine if you have fallen prey to one of the devil's schemes. One such way is to ask yourself if you aware of the counterfeits. If not, you are most likely deceived or under his influence. Almost everything God has put in place has been counterfeited by Satan. If that statement appears foreign to you, that means you are not aware of the many counterfeits. Here are a few examples: Christ, the church, Bibles, prophets, teachers, Israel (see Revelations 2:9 and 3:9), creation, joy, morality, etc.

Let's take salvation as an example. Are you aware of false salvation? The greatest counterfeit salvation scheme is perpetrated by the church itself. That is hard to believe, isn't it? It goes like this... The unsaved are asked to quote Romans 10:9 or a similar statement and once completed they are told they are saved. You said the magic words, abracadabra, you are saved, many have done just that and are convinced they are saved. The verses mentioned are correct but are slightly altered in their applications to produce false converts. Let's read the verses.

> *For, if you confess with your mouth that Jesus is Lord and believe in your heart that God raised him from the dead, you will be saved. For one believes with the heart and so is justified, and one confesses with the mouth and so is saved.* **Romans 10:9 – 10 (NAB)**

Two things need to be realized for the verses to be applied appropriately and for true salvation to be achieved. First, Jesus is Lord in the general sense. Most know this before they ever quote the verses. The key here is He must be Lord to you personally as well; you must surrender to his Lordship. What does that mean? It means He is Lord over your life, and He leads it. Second, belief must be with the heart. With the heart, it produces a transformation. Read Chapters "They See Without Seeing and Hear Without Hearing." Belief must penetrate the heart to be effective and cause a transformation. One can choose to take a different path but, in his heart, if he doesn't believe he will not follow it with his actions. The heart is the source to produce action.

> *These people draw near to Me with their mouth And honor Me with their lips, But their heart is far from Me. And in vain they worship Me, Teaching as doctrines the commandments of men.* **Matthew 15:8-9 (NKJV)**

When walking someone through salvation, these verses need to be explained in the fullest sense, or you will produce false converts. It should be explained what a true Christian is so no one will be misled. Let's pause for a second and think about the number of false converts the church has produced. Think about the seasoned and strong leaders who have carried out the deception. Think about its impact, this is shocking. That is just one deception or devil's scheme, altering the unadulterated truth by misapplying it. Simple, subtle, extremely effective and impactful. So subtle that biblically strong Christian leaders fall prey to it.

> *Not everyone that saith unto me, Lord, Lord, shall enter into the kingdom of heaven; but he that doeth the will of my Father which is in heaven.* **Matthew 7:21-23 (KJV)**

> **Verse 12, For our struggle, is not against flesh and blood, but against the rulers, against the authorities, against the powers of this dark world, and against the spiritual forces of evil in the heavenly realms. (KJV)**

We can surmise that humanity is not the source of the battle, but life experiences tell us humanity is an integral part of the battle. From this, we can deduce that the devil is influencing and manipulating humanity. We can also determine his influence is on a grand scale and it isn't confined to earth, but the heavens are included as well. It is a spiritual and physical battle and consequently, we must fight both in the physical realm and spirit.

We also know that the devil's subordinates are of different ranks. We need to understand each level, its authority, and its entity's power. Any great military leader will tell you to know your enemy, it is essential to success. From verse 11, we gather that his schemes are his primary battle weapon, and the schemes are played out by rulers, authorities, dark worldly powers, and spiritual beings under Satan's leadership. Rulers, authorities, and dark worldly powers are our human leaders posing as faithful and loyal world leaders. We are focusing on the pawns, while spiritual beings are manipulating governments, the media, organizations, school systems, etc. They are developing new ideologies, destroying foundational truths, societal bedrock, and truth itself. Your enemy isn't the chess pieces, it is the chess player. Also, do not overlook the spiritual component, prayer needs to be focused there as well. A Biblical study of spiritual warfare is needed, this is something preachers should make a primary task.

Verse 13, Therefore put on the full armor of God, so that when the day of evil comes, you may be able to stand your ground, and after you have done everything, to stand. (KJV)

The subcomponents of the armor are primarily built of defensive objects. You must put it all on, stand your ground, and do not retreat. Like any enemy, they attack at the weakest point, and when our defenses are down. So, when we don't have our armor on or we are lacking, we invite attacks.

The sword is our only offensive weapon, but it must be used effectively. The devil is relentless and without the use of the sword, there is nothing that's going to make him retreat. It requires you to be active, assertive, bold, and aggressive; or it is useless. The sword is our weapon of warfare. One thing is for sure, without the sword, there is no chance of victory.

A defensive-minded soldier who remains stationary never uses his sword. Satan doesn't bother him as long as he is spiritually stationary. The devil knows that if you put any animal in a corner and continuously beat him, he will eventually fight back no matter how passive he/she is.

As soon as he moves forward, Satan pushes him back, sometimes even gently. Every time he takes a few steps forward, he is struck by the enemy, so he retreats, never to overcome the trial or persecution, condemned to repeat it.

Here are a few examples of how this is played out in life: God has a ministry for you that will be abundantly fruitful and will build enormous treasures in heaven. It may require you to take a few Bible- related classes to get you prepared, or a small investment, willingness to spend five hours a week out in the ministry fields, join a men's/women's ministry, sacrifice your luxury car for a less expensive one, public speaking, the possibility of ridicule, etc. When one of these small requirements is present, Satan magnifies it and most just don't push to overcome the resistance. A gentle opposing push and most become ineffective. If we are not willing to push through a small roadblock, there is no way we can be an effective warrior. In America, we are sheltered from the sacrifices most of the world's Christians are enduring, losing all of their belongings, beatings, prison terms, and yes, their life. The sacrifices I have given up are embarrassingly small when compared to most of the world's Christians and not worth mentioning.

Verse 14, stand firm then, with the belt of truth buckled around your waist, with the breastplate of righteousness in place. (KJV)

It appears we must know the truth and stand firm in it, not deviating from the left or to the right or letting the world alter it. From Grace to You ministry. Truth is that which is consistent with the mind, will, character, and being of God. Truth is the self-expression of God.

> *I am the way and the truth, no one comes to the Father except through me.* **John 14:6 (NIV)**

Reality must be perceived through the lens of the Word. Any alteration of the Word is an attempt to alter the truth. So, when the scripture says put on the belt of truth, you are being commanded to know the truth, live it, and use it as a reference point to perceive reality. Any facts that contradict the word are false, anyone who presents an alternate view has fallen to deception. This holds for governments, organizations, media, political groups, etc. Also, spiritual beings are included.

Righteousness comes when we follow Christ's laws and decrees; this is a requirement for the battle. Righteousness is not earned; it is imputed to us through the sacrifice of Christ on the cross. How is righteousness a defensive weapon? Satan has no power or authority over us unless we give it to him. Sin is one avenue in which access to us is given to Satan. The world was under the leadership of Adam and Eve in the beginning, God gave them dominion over it. However, when Satan deceived them, he took control of them. The good thing is you can bring a stop to the damage by confessing the sin and repenting.

> *If we confess our sins, he is faithful and just and will forgive us our sins and purify us from all unrighteousness.* ***1 John 1:9 (NIV)***

> **Verse 15 and 16, and with your feet fitted with the readiness that comes from the gospel of**

peace. In addition to all this, take up the shield of faith, with which you can extinguish all the flaming arrows of the evil one. (NIV)

Don't let fear cause you to stumble. Live in a peace that is beyond human understanding, which God has provided. He will neutralize the power of Satan's arrows, but this requires faith.

Verse 17, Take the helmet of salvation and the sword of the Spirit, which is the word of God. (NIV)

Your faith in your salvation can't be wavery. You must know this without any doubt, otherwise, you will be vulnerable. The sword of the Word is your offensive weapon. Without it, you are standing in a defensive posture only. Without the Word, there is no way to get the devil to retreat. We know the devil is relentless. So, without the Word, you will face a relentless opponent with no offensive weapon.

Verse 18 and pray in the Spirit on all occasions with all kinds of prayers and requests. With this in mind, be alert and always keep on praying for all the Lord's people.

Prayer is a weapon we must employ, and we need to pray in the spirit. We need to pray for all the Lord's people.

Evaluate your current life: are you reactive or proactive to your life situations? Are you playing defense or are you on the offense? Let's look at two life scenarios, one reactive and the other proactive. Jack is the leader of his family, wife, and two kids. Jack gets up each day and prays for their protection. His kids come home from school and tell their father about the programs and classes the school will be presenting this year.

These programs are counter to his Biblical views. Jack and his wife engage the school's system will little success. So, Jack and his wife will educate their kids ahead of the counter programs the school will present to properly prepare the kids.

George, on the other hand, had already investigated the school programs and realized that his kid's exposure to them was unacceptable. George does not have a large income and can't afford to send both kids to private school. So, he sells his car with its payment and uses the monthly money saved to send one kid to a private school. George buys a twelve-year-old truck eye-sore with no luxury features and no payment. For the second kid, God provided a way for George: his wife could work with the neighbors for homeschooling. God provided the alternative because George and his family prayed for weeks for God to help his family not have to send his kids to the godless school.

George was proactive, in tune with the will of God, and properly prepared. George was willing to sacrifice for his kids. Jack, on the other hand, was reactive. **Jack's school system knows what he will be telling his kids, and they have a plan to counter** it. Plus, the school will act without his permission.

Jack thought by preparing his kids ahead of time for their exposure to the school system's curriculum he was successful. Satan's deceptions can be so complete that the Christian can even think he is winning until the blindsided checkmate is executed.

If the school system is depicted as a knight in our game of chess, we focus on capturing the knight or rendering it powerless. When we do this, we are being manipulated just like the pawns under his direct influence. Capturing the knight appears to be a step toward victory, but it leads to checkmate.

We may not be aware we are playing chess, for we are only concerned with the knight. It is our focus, and we may even be successful. If George tells Jack to execute a different move, Jack can't see it. George can't explain the overall strategy to Jack in a brief encounter because it took many hours of prayer, study, meditation, and the Holy Spirit's influence to get to the place he is in. Without the overall strategy comprehended, the Jack's in life have the big picture strategy, their moves appear to be illogical and even foolish.

This is the current state of the church: only a few have eyes that can see and ears that can hear. This isn't because they have greater intellect; no, it is because of their relationship with the Father, their God-given worldview, and their willingness to lay down their own wisdom and replace it with God's.

The state of the American Church is far worse than realized by most. The Chinese underground church prays for the American Church. The Chinese underground church lives with the possibility of death and incarceration daily. They secretly walk miles to attend services and spend days worshipping and praying. It isn't uncommon to be caught by the state and killed publicly, so they are battle-tested, seasoned Christians who do not compromise the Word. Their prayer for America is that we are persecuted for then the true Christians will surface, while the imposters reveal their true colors. The Chinese Christians believe that the American Church lives in a nation of freedom and we can help other Christians throughout the world. I believe this was true as well. This country was once a beacon of hope, a light on a hill. Now, I question if that is still true. At the very least, the light is fading.

If a secular-led military group would enter a large thousand-member or more American church facility with automatic weapons and request that all Christians walk to the front of the Church, the rest could leave. The members standing in front would be just a few, while the remaining imposters would make up excuses in their minds that would justify their cowardness and they would leave.

This is not true of the Chinese underground church; they would stand firm in the truth and lay down their lives for Christ. How do I know this? This is what they are currently doing, not only the adults, but the kids as well.

> Yea, and **all** that will live godly in Christ Jesus shall suffer persecution. **2 Timothy 3:12 (KJV)**

The weak Christian is reasoning his cowardness even now when he reads these words. What difference does it make to stand for Christ in this manner? It bears much fruit. Many of the soldiers who killed the Chinese church members, later gave their lives to Christ when confronted with this scenario, and other Christians who heard of their stance, questioned their own relationship with Christ. I know its impact on me has been dramatic. Rest assured; their sacrifice will not be ignored by the Father; their eternal reward is incomprehensible to our mortal eyes. I know I'm a member of this soft American church and would not put my bravery on the same level as the Chinese underground church. They get up each morning with the knowledge they may die for the Lord that day. They do not pray to get out of the situation, but to endure it. A different mindset than ours.

> Then Jesus said to his disciples, "Whoever wants to be my disciple must deny themselves and take up their cross and follow me. For whoever wants to save their life will lose it, but whoever loses their life for me will find it. **Matthew 16:24-25 (NIV)**

I fully understand why they pray that we fall under persecution, for under persecution, the church grows stronger.

Faith

I have heard many public figures, politicians, and everyday individuals proclaim they have faith, but some will proclaim the faith without attaching that faith to anything. Faith stands alone. If it isn't linked to someone or something then it isn't faith, it is just word salad. For example, if asked how you make it through the day considering your most recent loss, the response is, "I have faith." This is a meaningless statement. Faith alone can't bring comfort; it must be attached to something. Faith in God, in yourself, the universe, whatever. If you are not able to proclaim what you have faith in, then that faith is either shallow or nonexistent. I realize we make statements where we do not identify what our faith is in because it is said in the context of a larger conversation, or the hearer is well aware of your commitments. However, I'm speaking of individuals who state they have faith but never reveal who or what the faith is in.

That faith is valueless. In the same way, faith by itself, if it is not accompanied by action, is dead.

But someone will say, "You have faith; I have deeds."

Show me your faith without deeds, and I will show you my faith by my deeds. **James 2:17 (NIV)**

Faith motivates the receiver to work; at the very least, it should motivate one to identify the object of the faith. So, if faith without works is dead, and a proclaimer of faith that doesn't display works linked to said faith is a deceiver to others and possibly themselves. The scriptures say,

> *And without faith it is impossible to please God because anyone who comes to him must believe that he exists and that he rewards those who earnestly seek him. Hebrews 11:6 (NIV)*

Many proclaim to have faith in God but if works don't follow, their faith isn't genuine.

We have leaders who want to be your lord, and the tool they will use to lord over you is the government. This is why they are so adamantly working to replace God in every aspect of your lives, so when you are in need, you will call out to them. Therefore, communism and socialism are so attractive. If you are out of work, they will provide a program to help you until you are back on your feet; hospitalization, affordable insurance; education, free tuition; housing, section 8; income, California's proposed guarantee income program. The more the government provides the illusion of a safety net, the more subjects yield to their lordship. When the illusion is firmly set into place, you will hear these words, I have faith in the government, they will provide. The elite that is charged at the time will find great pleasure in the peoples' faith.

When good loving parents want their kids to become responsible citizens, they stop providing for all of their needs. They slowly teach their kids to become self-sufficient. If we have faith in God, we point them to God for their security.

Why? Because God is faithful. The government is not, history has painfully proven that. Anyone who seeks to make the government a safety net doesn't have adequate faith in God.

> *These people honor me with their lips,*
> *but their hearts are far from me.*
> *They worship me in vain;*
> *their teachings are merely human rules.*
> ***Matthew 15:8-7 (NIV)***

Wisdom

What is intangible, more valuable than gold and silver, free for the asking, available to all, distributed by God, accompanied by eternal treasures, and unlimited? Wisdom, of course. Prosperity follows wisdom, riches, and honor, keys to understanding parables and proverbs are all products of wisdom. The scripture says there is nothing you can desire to compare to her.

Wisdom comes from God; it is in the scriptures, and it is revealed through God's creation. But before wisdom can be appreciated, you must have a healthy fear of God. Without fear and respect for God, wisdom isn't available to the spiritually blind.

The heavens declare the glory of God;
the skies proclaim the work of his hands.
Day after day they pour forth speech;
Night after night they reveal knowledge.
They have no speech, they use no words; no sound is
heard from them.

Yet their voice goes out into all the earth, their words to the ends of the world. **Psalms 19:1-4 (NIV)**

When it comes to creation, it can be interpreted with and without the fear of God. A beaver builds a dam. An atheist sees an animal working foolishly and building dams due to random mindless effort. When a respecter of God sees a beaver building a dam, he asks why God designed beavers to build dams, and what benefits dam-up water brings to the ecosystem. He pursues the reasoning for building dams, and it opens a wealth of information that can be used in ecology as well as many other areas. He gains a vast amount of knowledge and wisdom from one simple observation.

When one realizes that God created different personality types and sets out to research why each type is needed, their function in society, their distribution ratios, etc. He begins on a journey that again brings a wealth of information and wisdom. He learns about God, His desires, His objectives, and His purposes for mankind.

These are just a couple of creation-related observations. When coupled with fear of God they bring wisdom. What about God's Word, God's special revelation?

God says men are born evil and are corruptible when given power. If one believes this, then he knows that communism doesn't work because it gives power to a few in control of many. This is why the American constitution is superior because it has three governing branches with leaders with limited terms. The purpose is to limit power, have checks and balances, and a method to remove corrupted individuals.

As stated earlier, the fear of God is the beginning of wisdom. This is why the theory of evolution is so dangerous. By removing God from the equation, you remove any chance of gaining wisdom. The theory of evolution is a product of Satan himself; it is a part of his scheme to destroy man. The destruction of the family, removal of prayer, shedding of innocent blood, and hiding of demonic possession under the guise of mental illness all are additional poisons aimed directly at God.

Here are a few characteristics of a wise man: he controls his tongue, he is slow to speak and quick to listen, he is God-centered, has a healthy respect for God, wise of Satan's schemes, puts on the armor of God, reads the Bible in its entirety, prays continuously, aware of God's mysteries, understands parables and greatly appreciates creation. These are just a few characteristics, but they are enough to point you to who is wise versus the imposter.

As I said earlier, the biggest obstacle to wisdom is one's exaggerated self-worth, their own wisdom. What I mean by this is the one who reads the first sentence of this paragraph who trusts in his own wisdom would think he is wise in Satan's schemes yet would have never done a study from the Bible on the schemes of Satan. He would believe he intuitively knows Satan's schemes. He has never put on the armor of God but feels he respects God. He can't understand a parable written by God for the wise, but he believes he is wise. The biggest obstacle to obtaining wisdom is our own belief in self.

Do not be wise in your own eyes; fear the LORD and shun evil. **Proverbs 3:7 (NIV)**

What Is Truth?

What is truth? Per the Oxford Dictionary, truth is that which is true or in accordance with fact or reality.

Deception is the action of deceiving someone. I give both definitions here because non-truth and deception are not the same things. In fact, you can deceive someone into making a wrong move by stating the truth. Therefore, you must distinguish between the two; if not, you may interpret scripture incorrectly.

Jesus states, "I am the way and the truth and the life. No one comes to the Father except through me." I believe Jesus is making a profound statement here when he refers to himself as the truth. He is the creator of all, the designer of both the intangible and the tangible. Therefore, all truth resides in him. We need to fully understand what he is stating here. Couple the truth with the giver of life and there isn't anything else and therefore Jesus is all 'n' all. The Alpha and the Omega, the Beginning and the End. Outside of Christ, there is no truth. Therefore, our opinions, perceptions, and values are worthless unless they are aligned with his. In fact, if we present anything outside of Jesus' truth, then we are lying, even if it is unintentional.

When we go to court and are sworn in, we must swear that we will tell the truth, the whole truth, and nothing but the truth. Why? Because partial truths and lack of knowledge can lead to deception. Satan uses these shortcomings to his advantage. Be aware of his schemes.

In Genesis 20:11-12, Abraham told a partial truth and therefore deceived another into believing something that wasn't true. This is important to understand for you can hear the truth and misapply it because you don't have the whole truth.

> *Abraham replied, "I said to myself, 'There is surely no fear of God in this place, and they will kill me because of my wife.' Besides, she really is my sister, the daughter of my father though not of my mother; and she became my wife. (NIV)*

So, Abraham's wife was his half-sister, so when he was confronted by Abimelek, Abraham was not lying when he stated she was his sister. However, it was not the whole truth. He should have also mentioned she was his wife as well. This omission was intentional to deceive Abimelek. So, it is not enough to tell a partial truth, we must tell the whole truth.

Matthew 4:5-7 Jesus was tempted by Satan in the wilderness. Satan presented to Jesus a truth. But its purpose was to deceive Jesus into testing the Father. So, the truth was stated but misapplied. This is where wisdom and the full knowledge of God's word were required to reveal the deception.

> *Then the devil took him to the holy city and had him stand on the highest point of the temple. "If you are the*

Son of God," he said, "throw yourself down. For it is
written:
"'He will command his angels concerning you, and they
will lift you up in their hands, so that you will not strike
your foot against a stone.'
Jesus answered him, "It is also written: 'Do not put the
Lord your God to the test. (NIV)

This is a good example of how we can pull truth from scripture and justify action, and it all seems correct. We can be aware of partial truth, and due to incomplete knowledge, the wrong action or conclusion is derived. Since we don't know what we don't know, we should always pray and be quick to listen to other brothers in Christ. Also, it is essential to have complete knowledge of scripture, the whole truth.

Those of you that are not privy to the scientific community may not be aware of this. There is a consorted effort to move absolute truth (God's truth) to relative truth. In this way, two people can have conflicting truths, but both can be correct. One can be a Buddhist and the other a Muslim. What is true for the Buddhist is the only truth for him, it is relative to his perspective.

I heard it put this way: one individual runs on a Microsoft Windows platform, while another boots up in Unix. So, what is true for the Windows environment may not be true for the Unix environment. Jesus, however, says He is the truth and that means His truth will be used to judge you. He is the giver of life, and His truth is the only one that counts.

Jesus answered, "I am the way and the <u>truth</u> and the
life. No one comes to the Father except through me.
John 14:6 (NIV)

The youth of this generation have embraced relative truth quite well. You hear conversations like this when preaching the gospel, "That is your truth, not mine, I have my own truth." Many of you will be surprised if you ask your kids questions concerning absolute truth, the public school system has programmed them this way.

Is the truth important? Consider this: when Jesus was standing before Pilate of Rome, he asked Jesus, Are you the King of the Jews?

> *Jesus answered, "You say that I am a king. In fact, the reason I was born and came into the world is to testify to the **truth**. Everyone on the side of truth listens to me." (NIV)*

Jesus makes it quite clear that he came to testify to the established truth. If you trust in him, you will accept it. There are other truths, but only one leads to the Father.

State Of The Mind

I'm living life just like everyone else, enjoying the things God has blessed me with, and loving my friends and relatives. Periodically, from deep within my heart, the spiritual condition of the world rises to the surface of my mind. Everything that I had been enjoying moments earlier seems trivial now. I know that the condition of most of the world is less than favorable and God's return is soon. It lays heavily on me I cry out to God, "What can I do, I'm wasting such precious time."

My worldly comforts and entertainment gradually faded into the background, replaced by duty and a strong sense of urgency. Eventually, I can't find rest in the world, I'm ready for battle. I need to preach God's Word, display the love He put in my heart, and articulate what He means to me. If I do not, I will implode. From peace to war and back again, this rollercoaster ride is my life; in between the extremes are my worldly responsibilities—work, home, family, society, etc. When performing my ministries, I feel at home. Preaching God's Word is my native tongue. Enjoying worldly things is short-lived and eventually turns to guilt, they give way to duty.

Within my core, my heart, I know there is a much greater walk for me. I've known it for most of my life. Now it occupies a significant portion of my attention. I have learned more Biblically within the last three years of my life than the rest, collectively. I feel like God is force-feeding me, my whole worldview has changed drastically. Recalling how I once understood the scriptures, in the past versus today's understanding, my past understanding is just a mere shadow of today. Not that the meaning of the word has changed. No, it is much fuller, richer. I feel like a warrior being prepared for battle, waiting for orders, and loyal to the death. I am so alone in a worldly sense, but spiritually, the comforter comforts me. He reminds me continuously, "I am with you, always."

I better understand His Words, and what He commands of each of us. Those who seek to live a Godly life will be persecuted. "Take up your cross and follow me, enter through the narrow gate, those who seek to save their lives will lose it, and those who lose their lives will save it."

In the context of a battle, these words have a different meaning when compared to the sterile American church version of Christianity. He tells us to put on the whole armor of God. Why? To prepare us for battle. Why does He use terms like battle and armor to describe it, so we will know what to expect. Our opponent seeks to kill, steal, and destroy. As a result, there will be injuries, difficulties, setbacks, loss of companions, and even death.

This world is a battlefield; carnage is everywhere, and it is extreme. Most of us have heard of the TV series called The Walking Dead, where zombies walk aimlessly through life. The Biblically-deceived bodies are like these zombies. Deceived bodies are marching aimlessly. These are the walking deceived, infecting more and more people as time progresses. The church is nowhere to be seen, for they are infected too.

There is one major difference between the Walking Dead series and our reality: few perceived the walking deceived for what they are, for they appear normal to each other. God's internal spirit living in the few uninfected, illuminates them. His Word calls them out, and their crude sounds are deafening. The deceived, their eyes are shut, blind and their ears are missing. They can't see or hear, but they speak proudly and boastfully, "Follow me, I have all of the answers." The deceived are constantly stumbling, falling, and injuring themselves; their injuries are too numerous to count. That doesn't remotely stop them from proclaiming, "Follow me." A few confront me saying, "You are going the wrong way, you fool," while they continue to fall and injure themselves. I attempt to point them in the right direction, I pull and push them, but since they can't see or hear, they ignore me. I pray for them, and God shines a bright light that illuminates the right path, but they hate the light for it exposes their condition. They gather in the dark and are comfortable there. I asked for help from the few who could partially see, and their responses were uninspiring. "I'm busy with my worldly task, I can't be bothered. Besides, it is not that bad. Don't get the deceived angry with us, I want their approval, just love them from afar."

I observe the deceived as they fight among themselves. They hate the sighted and can't tolerate them; the reds hate the greens, and the rich hate the poor, the left hates the right. They speak hatefully to each other, but they call it righteousness. They don't tolerate each other or the sighted, but claim they are tolerant themselves. They judge unmercifully, and in fits of rage, they kill their young and call it a right. Some of the deceived don't practice killing their young but they walk side by side with those that do, believing that it's adequate to make them good. They have no issue with their partnership.

Do not be deceived: "Bad company corrupts good morals." 1 Corinthians 15:33 (BSB)

I search for others who can see and hear and are not deceived. God says the path to him is narrow and only a few will find it. There are far fewer than expected, extremely difficult to find others. The deceived say they are on the right path, but that is impossible because they are in the majority. They do things that God hates, and God says no one who does these things will enter the kingdom. Some of the deceived refrain from doing the hated things, but again, they travel with the ones who do. They even select the damned for their leaders and see no conflict. The blood of the innocent stains their hands. The stains are only washed off under God's light, but they run from it. Therefore, I must preach the Word that God has put in my heart,

> *"Wherefore come out from among them, and be ye separate, saith the Lord, and touch not the unclean thing; and **I will receive you.**" 2 Corinthians 6:17 (KJV)*

Conclusion

Satan has launched a multiprong attack against all the pillars of Christianity, such as truth, wisdom, creation, family, government, logic, and reasoning, to name a few. He has made major sins that prevent access to the kingdom of heaven acceptable. He has labeled sin as good and good as sin. He has done this right in public sight and the Church has embraced it and, in some cases, even promoted it. The vast majority of us live in a sea of deception, unaware of their condition.

We live a life focused on worldly accomplishments that are only temporary, sacrificing eternal gifts in exchange. We emulate and idolize famous individuals hoping to earn admiration from people who live a life contrary to the will of God, and whose future is questionable.

In contrast, God said all efforts will be rewarded, even a small glass of water to a child for His namesake. If we suffer for His sake, the reward is greater than the suffering. If we die for Him, there is a crown waiting for us. There is no way to lose with God. In His life on earth as Jesus, He demonstrates how to live the perfect life for maximum results and maximum reward. He gives you everything you need to succeed. He says to start with nothing, His Holy Spirit will walk with you, guide you, and provide everything as you proceed through life. He told the rich man, if you want to be perfect, then go and give everything you have to the poor (start with nothing) and come follow me (I'll provide everything) (Matthew 19:21). From that point on, everything you do will be for Him because you left your life behind (maximum reward). And since you are following Him and He is your source for everything, maximum results.

He puts in our hearts His will and His laws so we can live a better life on Earth. His laws make life more enjoyable and prevent us from enduring unnecessary pain and suffering. But instead, Satan's subtle deceptions lead us down paths of destruction, pain, and hardship. God gives wisdom to all who ask, and a sound mind that is grounded in intuitive logic and exceptional reasoning abilities. Instead of utilizing God's gifts, we follow conclusions derived from faulty logic and poor reasoning. Some have reprobate minds, minds that can kill a baby in the womb with no remorse but will wail over an inadvertently crushed eagle egg because it is an endangered species. The reprobate mind can't perceive the contradiction. The reprobate mind defies logic, reasoning, and critical thinking skills. This mind can see design everywhere and be told by the scientific community though it appears to be design and meets the criteria of design, it evolved. Again, it can't perceive the flaw in the logic.

God gives us tools like cognitive dissonance, dreams, logic, sound reasoning, and critical thinking to reduce our chances of making mistakes. We ignore these tools, and we don't teach our kids to use them either. Our hearts are hardened due to unforgiveness, unmerciful judgment, and selfishness, The hardening heart leads to the inability to change, learn wisely, and see the truth.

In short, we live in a state of deception, deceived to the point we can't hear or see the truth. This condition is due to our sinfulness and yielding to the demands of the world.

Appendix

Scriptures marked AMP are taken from the Amplified Bible: Copyright © 2015 by The Lockman Foundation. Used by permission. lockman.org

Scriptures marked BB are taken from the Berean Standard Bible, public domain.

Scripture quotations from the Common English Bible. © Copyright 2011. All rights reserved. Used by permission. (www.CommonEnglishBible.com).

Scriptures marked KJV are taken from the King James Version, public domain.

Scriptures marked MSG are taken from the The Message: The Bible In Contemporary English: Copyright©1993, 1994, 1995, 1996, 2000, 2001, 2002. Used by permission of NavPress Publishing Group

Scripture marked NAB are taken from the New American Bible, revised edition © 2010, 1991, 1986, 1970 Confraternity

Acknowledgements

I want to thank my family for encouraging me to write this book and providing excellent feedback during the development process. During my youth, my atheist years, my family never rejected me or treated me with content. I was loved despite my foolishness. My mother contributed much to my path to salvation. She was firm in her belief, and never wavered, no matter what argument I would bring to her. My mother never finished high school, but she had a full grasp of the Word, looking back I see the Holy Spirit pouring much into her. We sometimes feel like we have an advantage because we are well-educated or have an above-average IQ. It can be a disadvantage; we tend to rely on our understanding instead of seeking out God's wisdom.

About The Author

C.J. Dakota's life has been a journey from atheism to a God-fearing believer of Christ. He had his pre-salvation worldview ripped apart by God. He learned so much over the years, but it was only a small fraction in the scheme of things. That knowledge has kept him humble and willing to learn.

His hope is that this book causes believers to understand that all can be easily deceived, and they should always be on guard against that weakness. There is only one truth and that is Christ. C.J. has been very blessed because he hasn't had too many difficulties in his life. And the few he had, he realized that overcoming trials brings strength and that was a blessing as well.

C.J. Dakota's prayer is that this book is the first of many, after the numerous eye-opening episodes in his life.

www.ingramcontent.com/pod-product-compliance
Lightning Source LLC
Chambersburg PA
CBHW051007140626
46546CB00016B/1031